James Joyce and Associated Image Makers

James Joyce

and

Associated Image Makers

By

Maria Elisabeth Kronegger

COLLEGE & UNIVERSITY PRESS · Publishers

NEW HAVEN, CONN.

Copyright © 1968 by

College & University Press Services, Inc.

Library of Congress Catalog Card Number: 68-22381

Grateful acknowledgment is made to the following publishers for per-
mission to quote from their publications: Charles Scribner's Sons for Ed-
mund Wilson, *Axel's Castle* (1931) and William York Tindall, *James Joyce:
His Way of Interpreting the Modern World* (1950); New Directions for
James Joyce, *Stephen Hero* (1955); and Random House, Inc., for James
Joyce, *Ulysses*, Modern Library Edition (1946). The Society of Authors,
London, England has also granted permission to quote from James Joyce,
Stephen Hero. Special acknowledgment is made to The Viking Press, Inc.,
for permission to quote from the following:

From *A Portrait of the Artist As a Young Man* by James Joyce
Copyright 1916 by B. W. Huebsch, 1944 by Nora Joyce
Copyright © 1964 by the Estate of James Joyce
All rights reserved
Reprinted by permission of The Viking Press, Inc.

From *Dubliners* by James Joyce
Originally published by B. W. Huebsch, Inc., in 1916
All rights reserved
Reprinted by permission of The Viking Press, Inc.

From *Finnegan's Wake* by James Joyce
Copyright 1939 by James Joyce, © 1967 by George Joyce and Lucia Joyce
Reprinted by permission of The Viking Press, Inc.

From *Exiles* by James Joyce
Copyright 1918 by B. W. Huebsch, 1946 by Nora Joyce
Copyright 1951 by The Viking Press, Inc.
Reprinted by permission of The Viking Press, Inc.

From *Collected Poems* by James Joyce
Copyright 1918 by B. W. Huebsch, Inc., 1946 by Nora Joyce
Reprinted by permission of The Viking Press, Inc.

MANUFACTURED IN THE UNITED STATES OF AMERICA BY
UNITED PRINTING SERVICES, INC.
NEW HAVEN, CONN.

TO MY PARENTS

Introduction

The existing commentaries on imagery in James Joyce's work provide many valuable insights into his multi-faceted prose. This study suggests a further expansiveness in the rich kingdom of Joycean imagery through a revelation of Joyce's imagistic kinship to Edgar Allan Poe and through a comparison of his patterns of imagery with those of representative impressionist, post-impressionist, and metaphysical painters.

Both in his concept of the universe and in his theory of the poet as a transcendental revealer, Joyce complements the aesthetic philosophy of Poe. While the imagery of the two artists takes its own individualistic directions, it derives in both cases from a mutual belief in the power of the will to shape external reality into anything that the imagination decrees. The Poe-like vision of Joyce's work is evidenced in this fundamental concept of the artistic pursuit as a fictive translation of experience and of the universe.

With the French symbolists (Baudelaire, Rimbaud, Mallarmé), whose indebtedness to Poe is a critical commonplace, Joyce maintained that the artist's concern must be to attain a mystical insight into supraterrestrial reality beyond the world of sensation. Both Poe and Joyce isolate, fragment, and transpose elements of common experience in strikingly similar imagistic patterns. To dislocate and recombine elements of visual experience is for them an intuitive process whereby the elements of the natural universe may become symbolic revelations of transcendental reality. Fragmentary imagery becomes a means for symbolizing the broken universe of man, time, and space. At the same time, by means of a reassimilation of broken images into ordered geometric forms, Joyce and Poe attempt to give a spiritual coherence to life and the universe.

The use of circular and cyclic imagery provides a symbolic synthesis unbounded by the exigencies of time and space. In the works of both authors there appears a steady evolution from the microcosmic circle to ever larger circles that expand in the general universe and relate finally all existence to the cycles of the macrocosmos.

For these artists the source of both chaos and spiritual unity is in the mind; therefore, the levels of consciousness are not simply isolated phenomena. They are, rather, symbolic revelations of a transcendental import which take their shape in the mind in terms of complex combinations of experiences in the physical world. Their protagonists, unable to will order to the external or unconscious experience, are caught up in a paralysis which cuts across their physical, intellectual, and spiritual existence. This atrophy of will power is conducive to an urge for wild sensations or acts of perverseness. Both authors recognize in the paralysis of the individual and his consequent frenzy the death of meaning in the world.

Like Poe, Joyce tries to counteract this death of meaning in the world by ascribing an evocative power to the word. A word engenders a universe. Like a musical note or a pure color, the word takes on a power which not only serves as an identifying sign, but becomes a dynamic symbol which both participates in and evokes the idea itself. Through the word *per se* a new and coherent reality arises.

Poe, Joyce, and the impressionist, the post-impressionist, and metaphysical painters share in the desire to release the reality which is concealed behind the screen of the commonplace. As such, they are the forerunners of surrealism. In contradistinction from the surrealists, however, Poe and Joyce do not attempt a liberation of the subconscious by an extreme separation of this level of experience from the levels of intellect and reason. They aim with the impressionists at a unification of impression and effect. Like the impressionists they aim at a totality of mood. But unlike them, they do this through an intricate pattern of detail. And Joyce recognizes more clearly than Poe an under-lying significance which detail lends beyond the creation of artistic effect. While both artists recognize that the order of their worlds obtains from within the realm of pure subjectivism, Joyce creates out of empirical formlessness a new world of a more complex philosophical import than Poe does.

Nevertheless, the method which Joyce employs is basically that of Poe. Through the French writers and painters the effects of Poe's aesthetics are translated into a philosophy of life as well as of art. Joyce appreciated Poe's imagery and aesthetics in three ways: (1) by direct contact, (2) through the Poe revival in Ireland, Britain, France and the United States, and (3) through the transmitted effect on modern painters. This study presents evidence of this relationship through a detailed comparative analysis of basic patterns of imagery in the two writers and of the Joycean imagery with the methods of representative painters whose dominant motifs reveal an ideational indebtedness trace-able to Poe.

Contents

CHAPTER ONE

External Evidence of the Presence of Poe and the French Symbolists in Joyce

> The poet is the intense centre of the life of his age to which he stands in a relation than which none can be more vital. He alone is capable of absorbing in himself the life that surrounds him and of flinging it abroad again amid planetary music.
>
> *Stephen Hero*

There is a considerable body of evidence that James Joyce was acquainted with the work of Edgar Allan Poe and that some of his most important artistic devices derived from the American writer. It is a commonplace that Joyce had an encyclopedic mind and that his sources of style and content embrace a wide range. Yet his indebtedness to numerous writers upon whom Poe had a direct and often profound impact suggests that an examination of the parallels between their aesthetic and stylistic concepts and practices may provide a useful key to the further understanding of Joyce.

There is very little proof that Joyce knew Poe directly. Joyce designates Poe in his "Essay on Mangan" as "the high priest of most modern schools,"[1] even though Mangan has surpassed him in the use of musical echo in poetry.

Throughout his work, Joyce makes frequent allusions to America. As early as "Dubliners" America is often mentioned. Besides, there are specific evocations of an "Allan Line going out to

Canada,"[2] a "Bog of Allen,"[3] and a "Hill of Allen,"[4] suggesting
Allan. Further, in "The Dead" and in *Ulysses* Joyce mentions
"Usher's Island,"[5] perhaps in allusion to Poe's protagonist Usher.
With the opening pages of *Finnegans Wake* Dublin is located
on an American river in Georgia.[6] There is mention of a Mo-
zambique Channel, considered as the longest river in America.[7]
Geographically, the action often takes place in a North Richmond
Street[8] or in Norse Richmound.[9] A North Richmond Street exists
in Dublin, yet suggests at the same time Poe's city of Richmond.
In *Finnegans Wake* Joyce uses the same words in allusion to
Poe as did once Baudelaire, when exclaiming: "Mon semblable,
mon frère."

> We were in one class of age like to two clots of egg. I
> am most beholding to him, my namesick, as we sayed it
> in our Amharican, through the Doubly Telewisher. . . .
> I am no scholar but I loved that man who has africot
> lupps with the moonshane in his profile, my shemblable!
> My freer! I call you my half-brother because you in
> your soberer otiumic moments remind me deeply of my
> natural saywhen brothel in feed, hop and jollity. . . .[10]

There is a reference in *Ulysses* to an "American cousin" and to
"Pue's Occurrences,"[11] suggesting Poe's occurrences. The name
of Poe is mentioned only in connection with "Poe's Toffee's Di-
rectory"[12] in *Finnegans Wake*. Poe's works "Eureka," "The Conversation of Eiros and Charmion," and "The Mystery of Marie
Roget" Joyce evokes in *Finnegans Wake*. He makes an allusion
to "Eureka," saying: "tomkin about your lief eurekason and his
undishcovery of americle; . . ."[13] Joyce suggests Eiros and
Charmion, speaking of a "cousin charmian" and "Erio";[14] and
he evokes Marie Roget, Poe, and Allan in the sentence: "Since
Allan Rogue loved Arrah Pogue."[15]

These seem to be the major direct indications that Joyce knew
Poe and admired him. More significant, however, is the indirect
indebtedness to his American "cousin."

However indirect the influence of Poe upon Joyce, two major
literary developments, both of which are indebted to Poe, were

coincidental with Joyce's own artistic development. The first of these was the Poe revival in England which occurred at about the time Joyce was reaching his maturity in Dublin. This interest in Poe was expressed by such contemporaries of Joyce as Yeats, Wilde, Swinburne, Symons, Rossetti and George Moore. The second and more important influence was the French symbolist movement which is universally recognized as having been heavily indebted to Poe. In addition to these two mainstreams of interest in Poe which occurred during Joyce's formative years, there are many additional indications of Joyce's probable contact with the work of Poe. Even such diverse writers as Ezra Pound and A. Conan Doyle, both of whom were instrumental in Joyce's ideational development, were interested in the contemporary flowering of Poe's art and theory.

A detailed account of the English revival of Poe during the late nineteenth century is presented by Harro Heinz Kühnelt in his *Die Bedeutung von Edgar Allan Poe in der englischen Literatur*.[16] In this dissertation Kühnelt delineates the nature of Poe's influence in the works of Swinburne, Wilde, Yeats and others of the English *fin de siècle* group. Yeats, for example, who is generally recognized to be the foremost English poet of the period, employs the themes of hypnosis and transmigration of souls in *A Vision*; he conceives of art as a means of escape into a sphere of eternal beauty and harmony; he concludes that the only reality is the world of dreams, for this is the source of both beauty and harmony; and his absorption in occultism and spiritualism generally are motive forces in his poetry.[17] All of these traits are to be found in Poe. Yeats, long a friend of Joyce, is known to have introduced Joyce to Arthur Symons, Pound, and the French symbolists. It seems not unlikely that this close association between Joyce and Yeats, the latter of whom resembles Poe in so many respects, produced between them discussions of the American writer and his startling aesthetic and spiritualistic theories. Certainly the influence of Yeats on Joyce is clear; for example, *Finnegans Wake* is indebted to *A Vision* in many respects.[18]

Poe's ideas were doubtless further promoted in Joyce's thought by Oscar Wilde and Algernon Charles Swinburne. Wilde and his works are frequently quoted throughout Joyce's novels. Wilde's aesthetic theory is similar to that of Poe; he considers all art to be perfectly "useless." As Edward Shanks has remarked, Wilde's aesthetic position is "the logical culmination of Poe's distinction between poetry and truth and of the endeavor of all decadents to prove that the poet stands apart from the common needs of mankind."[19] The similarity between the Poe-Wilde position and Joyce's own attitude is striking: Joyce's self-conscious theory of artistic creation which is elaborated in the climax of "A Portrait of the Artist" depicts the artist as an outcast of society for the sake of his creation. Similarly, after having read (in 1906) Wilde's *The Picture of Dorian Gray*, Joyce grasps something of the concepts of synaesthesia and of the fantastic which Wilde had inherited from Poe:

> "Some chapters," says Gorman, "are like Huysmans' catalogued atrocities: lists of perfumes and instruments. The central idea is fantastic. Dorian is exquisitely beautiful and becomes awfully wicked—but never ages. His portrait ages."[20]

Similarly, Swinburne, whose works Joyce read, shows an aspect of Poe's aesthetics which is to be found also in Joyce's art, an emphasis upon the artistic powers of music. Swinburne remarks that only once

> has there sounded out of it all [American literature] one pure note of original song worth singing, and echoed from the singing of no other man; a note of song neither wide nor deep, but utterly true, rich, clear, and native to the singer; the short, exquisite music, subtle and simple and sombre and sweet, of E. Poe.[21]

It is significant that in discussing aesthetics Joyce often refers to Conan Doyle, for the latter was much impressed by Poe, especially by his theories of ratiocination. In "A Philosophy of Composition" Poe compares the composition of poetry to the finding of a cryptogram. Both Doyle's stories and Joyce's epiphanies[22] reveal a structural indebtedness to a kind of mathematical formulation of images in relationship to basic themes. The method reveals the conscious imposition of the artist's will and design upon his material. This careful, contrived approach to the work of art is prominent in all three artists, but none succumbs to a complete mechanization of the structure of the work. Poe's dictum that it is not simply the structure but rather the movement of the psyche which determines the quality of the work is subscribed to by Joyce. He would have agreed with Poe that "it is in Music" in which "the soul most really attains . . . the creation of supernal Beauty."[23]

Not all of the contemporary reactions to Poe which Joyce doubtless encountered were enthusiastic. While it is unlikely that Pound's critical remarks on Poe had any significant effect on Joyce's work, since Pound came to England in 1913,[24] his objections reveal the extensiveness of Poe's influence on the English writers of the *fin de siècle*. Pound criticizes the adoption of Poe as a model poet. Emphasizing that Poe's verse was second only to Whitman's, he protested the forming of the English Poe cult which had grown up from Mallarmé's translation of "The Raven."[25] Pound also recognized that it was not simply Mallarmé's interest in Poe that produced the subsequent English revival, but also that Arthur Symons was a key figure in the establishment of a "cult of Poe."[26]

Symons was perhaps the key figure not only in the English revival of Poe but in making the Poe influence available to Joyce. Symons considers Poe as a major source of inspiration for Charles Baudelaire, Villiers de L'Isle Adam, Stéphane Mallarmé, Paul Verlaine and Joris-Karl Huysmans. All these writers, he maintains, accepted Poe's aesthetics and imagery as a basis for their creativity. Joyce read Symons' *The Symbolist Movement in Literature* in 1899.[27] Poe's influence on the French symbolists is presented with such emphasis therein that Joyce, who wanted to understand their poetry and prose, might well have been stimulated to investigate further the source of their inspiration.

Symons was more interested in Huysmans than in any other symbolist of the time as Max Wildi has shown in his dissertation:

> Über keine Gestalt, nicht einmal über Verlaine, der ihm [Symons] doch im Leben näher stand, hat er so oft und so eindringlich geschrieben. . . . Ein entscheidender Zug muss ihn mit Huysmans verknüpfen, wenn dessen Wandlungen für ihn so tiefes Interesse haben. Dieser Zug liegt in der Eigenart des Sinnenlebens. . . . In diesem Mitschwingen des ganzen Sensoriums und in der bangen Gebundenheit an dessen Reaktionen ist A. Symons mit Huysmans verbunden.[28]

Stimulated by Symons' interest in synaesthesia that he found best expressed by Huysmans, Joyce read À Rebours rather early, and Là-Bas in 1901.[29]

As an example of a direct relationship between Poe and symbolist writing which in turn affected the work of Joyce, Symons discusses in detail Huysmans' À Rebours.[30] Symons recognizes that Des Esseintes, the main character of the book, had with Poe "the instinctive sympathy which drew Baudelaire to the enigmatically perverse Decadent of America."[31] When Des Esseintes is in a winecellar in Paris he recalls Poe's tales of horror: "The winecellar is crowded with Englishmen: . . . as he drinks his Amontillado, the recollection of Poe puts its new horror into the good-humoured faces about him."[32] Having read Poe's works, Des Esseintes admits that "toute la littérature lui semblait fade après les terribles philtres importés de l'Amérique."[33]

The aesthetic withdrawal of Des Esseintes had previously been idealized by Poe. Des Esseintes resembles Roderick Usher in his life of luxury and isolation. He wishes to hide himself away, far from the world, in some retreat, where he might deaden the sound of the loud rumbling of inflexible life. Des Esseintes mentions Poe thirteen times and is in possession of Poe's complete works in editions bound in leather and decorated in vivid colors. Almost every artificial detail of his shut-in paradise is borrowed from Poe's interiors, as in the disordered preoccupation with what Usher himself called "a morbid acuteness of the senses." Des Esseintes and Poe are mostly interested in sensations "and chiefly the visual sensations."[34] For this reason Des Esseintes admires Baudelaire who shares a common interest in intense thoughts with Poe:

> [Baudelaire] s'était engagé à travers des galeries abandonnées ou inconnues, avait abouti à ces districts de l'âme òu se ramifiaient les végétations monstrueuses de la pensée.
>
> Là, près de ces confins où séjournent les aberrations et les maladies, le tétanos mystique, la fièvre chaude de la luxure, les typhoïdes et les vomitos du crime, il avait trouvé, couvant sous la morne cloche de l'Ennui, l'effrayant retour d'âge des sentiments et des idées.[35]

Poe's concept of the strange is an element that Symons finds in Huysmans: "Considering within himself, he realized that a work of art, in order to attract him, must come to him with that quality of strangeness demanded by E. A. Poe."[36] To Poe there was no beauty without strangeness. Joyce must have read in *À Rebours* the concept of the strange as formulated by Des Esseintes in Poe-like terms:

> En se sondant bien, néanmoins, il comprenait d'abord que, pour l'attirer, une oeuvre d'art devait revêtir le caractère d'étrangeté que réclamait E. Poe, mais il s'aventurait volontiers plus loin, sur cette route et appelait des flores byzantines de cervelle et des déliquescences compliquées de langue; il souhaitait une indécision troublante sur laquelle il put rêver, jusqu'à ce qu'il la fît, à sa volonté, plus vague ou plus ferme selon l'état momentané de son âme. Il voulait en somme, une oeuvre d'art et pour ce qu'elle était par elle-même et pour ce qu'elle pouvait permettre de lui prêter.[37]

It is signifcant that Poe's concept of the strange, directing the dreams of Des Esseintes, became one of Joyce's leading devices in the use of images.

Further similarities between Joyce's work and Symons' de-

scriptions of the symbolists may be found in the latter's statement that rhetoric, exteriorities, and descriptions ought to be
replaced by magical evocations of more beautiful things. Through
symbols, an affirmation of universal analogies, the soul of things
may be made more visible.[38] This concept directs Joyce's formulation of what he called epiphanies. Joyce's epiphany is the sudden showing forth of the individual soul in an incident, a scene,
a gesture, a phrase, a coincidental set of circumstances. The
individual essence might be revealed by a detail or an object to
which it has only a fortuitous relation.

What made Poe particularly acceptable to the French and
what interested Joyce especially was their interest in his aesthetic
theory. The theory of suggestion that influenced Joyce deeply
does not stem directly from Mallarmé, but from Poe, although,
on the contrary, David Hayman's book was to prove:

> C'est aussi dans les *Poètes Maudits*[39] que Joyce trouva
> la première référence à l'oeuvre suggestive par excel-
> lence, "l'oeuvre pure" mallarméenne (d'après laquelle
> il allait écrire *Finnegans Wake*). . . .[40]

In 1899 Joyce also read Symons' *Symbolist Movement* with
the remark that Mallarmé's aesthetic aim was: "To evoke, by
some elaborate, instantaneous magic of language, without the
formality of an after all impossible description; to be, rather
than to express."[41] One of the sources of this theory might be
Poe's famous theory that a poem is "that class of composition in
which there lies beneath the transparent uppercurrent of meaning
an under or suggestive one."[42] Therefore the images of symbolist
and impressionist writers must be defined through indeterminate
incidents, through images that suggest rather than denote, that
do not name things but create their atmosphere. Camille Mauclair
affirms that the theory of suggestion derived from Poe:

> De cette dernière maxime [the theory of suggestion]
> est peut-être sortie la théorie de *l'allusion* qui fut une
> des armatures de la poétique de Mallarmé, et par là du
> symbolisme français. Il suffit de lire cette phrase avec

attention pour reconnaître que si Poe s'est diverti à
présenter la *Genèse d'un Poème* sous la forme d'un jeu
mathématique, avec *cynisme* en face des amateurs de
délire, comme dit Baudelaire, il a pourtant respecté la
part mystérieuse du subconscient.[43]

We assume, then, that Joyce got from Symons the notion that
Poe broke with the rhetorical tradition for the sake of suggestion.
By suggestion the writer conveys a multiplicity of meanings.
This is a quality of Villiers' *Tales of the Grotesque and Arabesque*
that rival those of Poe, as Symons points out.[44] Joyce accepted
Poe's device of suggestion, as we know from the Irish writer's
remark to Frank Budgen, "I want the reader to understand
always through suggestion rather than direct statement."[45] Poe
also developed the familiar symbolist doctrine

that indefiniteness is an element of the true music [of
poetry]—I [Poe] mean of the true musical expression
. . . a suggestive indefiniteness of meaning with a view
of bringing about a definiteness of vague and therefore
of spiritual effect.[46]

Symons restates how Poe heightens these suggestive meanings
by "the vast force of an accompaniment in music. . . . With each
note of the lyre is heard a ghostly, and not always a distinct, but
an august and soul-exalting *echo*."[47] In fact, for Poe and for
Joyce, the highest reaches of generic poetry are to be found not
in the poem itself, but in music.

As already mentioned, Joyce refers to Poe in his "Essay on
Mangan" (1901) as "the high priest of most modern schools,"
even though Mangan had surpassed him in the use of musical
echo in poetry.[48] It is evident that Joyce, in the foosteps of Poe's
tradition, with the help of the French symbolist poets, developed
the literary devices of suggestion and of musical effects to
perfection.

Besides the attempt to make the effects of poetry approximate
those of music, Joyce wished to purify the words of the tribe.
While reading the *Poètes Maudits* of Paul Verlaine, Joyce found

in this edition the sonnet on Poe, "Le Tombeau d'Edgar Poe," by Mallarmé with the device to give "un sens plus pur aux mots de la tribu";[49] this characteristic that Mallarmé ascribes to Poe, was also his own and became one of Joyce's leading devices. This purification of language Joyce achieves by synaesthesia, by autonomous images full of discursive content and by evoking the images with the magic of a musical language in symphonic arrangement. Mallarmé, the most faithful Poe scholar, who learned English only to better understand Poe, based his life's work on the ideologies of Poe. Symons in 1899 highly praised the translations of Poe by Mallarmé, because Poe's poems and prose

> are among the most beautiful poems written in our time, prose which has all the subtlest qualities of prose, that, quitting the abstract point of view, we are forced to regret the fatal enchantments, fatal for him, of theories which are so greatly needed by others, so valuable for our instruction, if we are only a little careful in putting them into practice.[50]

This must have been a very stimulating criticism for such a young student as Joyce was, when he read it in 1899, at the age of seventeen.[51] In March, 1902, Joyce read Mallarmé's *Divagations* and the rest of Mallarmé's work during his stay in Trieste, between 1904 and 1914, while working on *Stephen Hero* and *A Portrait of the Artist as a Young Man*.[52]

Symons, when discussing Mallarmé's aesthetics in *The Symbolist Movement* which Joyce read, mentions also Poe's theory that no long poem was ever written and that the age of epics had passed. These are some reasons for our assumption that Joyce learned to know Poe's tales and poetry by his close study of Mallarmé's work and by the comments that he gathered on Poe while reading Symons' introduction to the symbolist movement.

It is an acknowledged fact that Flaubert influenced Joyce. Joyce turned to Flaubert as he did to the symbolist writers, because they showed him a way to express reality not by realistic details, but by symbols based on metaphysical concepts in the way Poe conceived them. Joyce had learned to use the impressionist and symbolist techniques of expression in the short interval between the first and last drafts of *Dubliners*. The first symptoms of the shift from realistic to impressionistic and symbolistic details is indicated in *Stephen Hero* in which Stephen rejects all the "portrayals of externals" and says that the artist must free "the image from the mesh of defining circumstances chosen as the most exact for it in its new office."[53] Flaubert's realistic details have had less influence on Joyce than Flaubert's metaphysical concepts. Joyce viewed all reality through a metaphysic of art alone. George Moore supports this view: "If the artist is a man for whom the visible world exists . . . then Joyce is essentially a metaphysician; for he is less concerned with the seeing eye than with the thinking mind."[54]

When Joyce was back in Paris in 1920, the American Ezra Pound introduced him to the *cénacles* of the *Mercure de France* and of the review *This Quarter*. There Joyce made the acquaintance of Paul Valéry, the Frenchman who was so deeply impressed by Poe's theories of pure poetry and by Poe's "Eureka." Joyce had met André Gide too. Gide considers Poe as one of the originators of the interior monologue.[55] Edouard Dujardin in *Le Monologue Intérieur* mentions that "certains contes de Poe (entre autres: "Le Coeur Révélateur" et d'admirables poèmes de Browning) . . . n'en restent pas moins à mes yeux de parfaites, d'indispensables réalisations du genre monologue intérieur."[56] It seems that Dujardin based his form of the interior monologue on some aspects of Poe's by which Mallarmé and Rimbaud among other symbolists definitely had been inspired.

The fact that Joyce wrote an essay on Mangan in 1902 is significant for two reasons: (1) Joyce discovers in Mangan the use of the artifice of reiterated refrain, whose generally acknowledged founder has always been considered to be Poe; (2) spiritual kinship existed between Mangan and Poe, for Mangan, the artist, spiritually exiled like Poe, is in revolt against actuality and flees from common reality to dreams. The Irish Mangan resembles Poe, who is also of Irish descent, by the life he led and by his literary expression.[57] This fact reveals anew Joyce's sympathy with all that was written in terms of Poe's aesthetics.

All these individual English and French influences combined to create the climate of Joyce's formative years: the *fin de siècle* and the opening of the twentieth century.

The major role in introducing Joyce to Poe's work was played by Symons: Symons refers, as we have seen, many times to Poe. Symons' discussion of the French symbolists stimulated Joyce to read their original works. The French symbolists admired the work of Poe to such an extent that they perfected Poe's aesthetic theories and motifs, which Joyce absorbed while reading them.

The best evaluation of this Poe influence in England and France is given by Edmund Wilson:

> It is not usually recognized that writers such as W. B. Yeats, James Joyce, T. S. Eliot, Gertrude Stein, Marcel Proust and Paul Valéry represent the culmination of a self-conscious and very important literary movement; and even when we have become aware that these writers have something in common, that they belong to a common school, we are likely to be rather vague as to what its distinguishing features are.
>
> . . . .
>
> What made Poe particularly acceptable to the French, however, was what had distinguished him from most of the other Romantics of the English-speaking countries: his interest in aesthetic theory. . . . And it was in France that Poe's literary theory, to which no one seems to have paid much attention elsewhere, was first studied and elucidated. So that, though the effects and devices of symbolism were of a kind that was familiar in English and though the Symbolists were sometimes indebted to English literature directly—the Symbolist Movement itself, by reason of its origin in France, had a deliberate self-conscious aesthetic which made it different from anything in English.[58]

In conclusion, an inquiry into Joyce's work and methods reveals his indirect knowledge of and dependence upon Edgar Allan Poe and the French symbolists in at least the following

respects, and proves that he relies on them for the perfection of
the following concepts:

1. Suggestion, a literary device that he derives via Mallarmé
   from Poe.
2. Musical effects and the use of refrain.
3. Analogy as a basic means of showing the connection between physical, spiritual and psychological life.
4. The interior monologue.
5. Synaesthesia.
6. Ratiocination and the epiphany.

These and other similarities will be included in the discussions
of the parallel patterns of imagery in Joyce and Poe in the suc-
ceeding chapters. We should not forget that

> Joyce, although he had already written in the same
> mood before the publication of *Du Côté de chez Swann*,
> had, from childhood, been saturated with French litera-
> ture, and had lived in Paris. Also he was an Irishman,
> and this made him more ready to accept inspiration
> from France than from England—indeed there is very
> little of the English tradition in his writings.[59]

All these artistic devices, however, constitute only a minimum
portion of what Joyce actually assimilated from Poe's work. In
a closer comparison of Joyce's and Poe's imagery we discover
new aspects of seeing and understanding their world picture.
This world picture, strangely enough, discloses to us the world
of the impressionist and metaphysical painters, the forerunners
of the surrealists. The fragmentation of images starts a movement of dissolution of the solid world of appearances. This I
would like to discuss in the following chapter.

CHAPTER TWO

Fragmentary and Circular Imagery

The Fragmentation of Images

Since Poe and Joyce are trying to assimilate reality spiritually, their power of imagination comes into play in the observation of the external world. In Poe's and Joyce's work the world of appearances is broken up into fragments. They discover an objective significance in cracks, in fissures, in broken objects, cracked looking glasses, ragged mountains, and crumbling houses. These broken images of the external world are projections of the minds and moods of the protagonists. Yet beyond the appearance of these images of a broken world, Poe and Joyce find harmonies of universal correspondences. Therefore they emphasize the inseparability of the formal, intellectual and emotional aspects of the image, symbol, or epiphany. The names of exterior objects become an instantaneous direction for the mind of their protagonists to travel between their ideas and their externalization. Thus, for both Poe and Joyce, every state of mind has a readily known representation. A new order arises that springs only from the mind of the artist.

Poe and Joyce reveal in this new order a superior reality. They render this superior reality by images of pure geometrical forms that at the same time reflect the basic structure of the universe. Therefore Poe and Joyce combine the images of squares, angles, spheres, circles, curves, triangles, lines, cones, cubes, pyramids, boxes, spirals and corkscrews with one another, because these images are figurations of essential mathematical properties from which the necessary conclusions can be drawn. Hence, Poe and Joyce project into their work, on the one hand, their moods and perceptions of a broken universe and, on the other hand, while striving to pierce to the significant heart of everything, they break the external world into a series of detached aspects that they regroup in images of geometrical order and form. For these reasons I propose to compare the following features of Poe's and Joyce's imagery in two sections: (1) the dissolution of individuals and vivisection; (2) imagery of geometrical figurations.

Poe and Joyce illustrate in their imagery a perpetual crumbling of individuals, who, like mountains, are slowly eroded into the plain of uniformity.

The conclusions of "Narrative of A. Gordon Pym" or "Berenice" by Poe and "The Dead" by Joyce affirm this viewpoint. Poe's "Berenice" depicts how reality breaks up into fragments and how social relations between the protagonists fall apart by their mental and physical breakdown. The physical and moral dissolution of Berenice is contrasted with the mental and spiritual degeneration of the narrator. Berenice, a person of action, undergoes an exterior breakdown by epilepsy, by "startling changes wrought in the *physical* frame of Berenice!"[1] The narrator's deterioration is seen as an inner, mental one, in which the "sunlight of [his] reason" is gradually submerged in the shadow of his irrationality. The end underscores this breakdown. In broken sentences a servant tells Egaeus of a violated grave. With a horrible cry Egaeus seizes a box, but in his weakness and excitement he drops it and the box, in falling, scatters instruments of dental surgery over the floor, mingling the frightful sound of metal with the accursed objects of his hallucination.

The story depicts the breakdown of the rational order. The physical and mental collapse of both Egaeus and Berenice is mirrored in the falling material objects. Speaking in general terms, Jung designates the dissolution of a personality as a very significant trait of modern art:

> Die Verhunzung von Schönheit und Sinn durch groteske Sachlichkeit oder durch ebenso groteske Unwirklichkeit ist beim Kranken eine Folgeerscheinung der Zerstörung seiner Persönlichkeit, beim Künstler aber schöpferische Absicht. Ferne davon in seiner Kunstschöpfung den

Ausdruck der Zerstörung seiner Persönlichkeit zu er-
leben und zu erleiden, findet der moderne Künstler im
Zerstörerischen geradezu die Einheit seiner künstler-
ischen Person.[2]

Poe presents this type of dissolution in "Loss of Breath":
a doctor discovers after dissecting a person that she is reani-
mated. This image, transposed into the terms of the artist, means
that the dissection or dissolution of a personality is necessary in
order to re-create unity in a person whose life becomes more
real after the dissection. In "Metzengerstein" Poe depicts the
dissolution of personalities, revealing the horror of living death
that in Joyce's episode of the "Wandering Rocks" is presented in
a group of individuals whose social relationships had gradually
decayed and dissolved.

Beside the picture of the living death of a society, Poe and
Joyce relate the dissolution of a personality to the dissolution of
its environment. Poe relates the decay of the palace of Usher as
it is pictured in the tarn to the dissolution of its inhabitants.
Joyce, similarly, depicts in "A Portrait of the Artist" the analogy
between the decay of the inorganic world and the dissolution of
an individuality:

> He [Stephen] smiled to think that it was this disorder,
> the misrule and confusion of his father's house and the
> stagnation of vegetable life, which was to win the day
> in his soul. Then a short laugh broke from his lips as
> he thought of that solitary farmhand in the kitchen gar-
> dens behind their house. . . .[3]

Poe and Joyce stress in these images the fragmentary lives of
individuals whose conditions of health are reflected in the objects of nature, yet who live solitarily apart from human society.
This fragmentary existence of human beings is intensely felt
when the protagonists are victims of a fall, and, awakening from
their dreams, find themselves "amid the fragments of a miscel-
laneous dessert, intermingled with a newspaper, some broken
glass and shattered bottles, and an empty jug . . ."[4] or see "both

above and below . . . visible fragments of vessels, large masses
of building-timber and trunks of trees, with many smaller articles,
such as pieces of house furniture, broken boxes, barrels and
staves."[5] These images embody the isolation and frustration of
the protagonists. It is a type of image that Bloom perceives in
his vision of Nova Hibernia of the future where the inhabitants
are lodged in barrels and boxes and where Dublin's walls
collapse.

> Mr. Bloom walked unheeded along his grove by sad-
> dened angels, crosses, broken pillars, family vaults,
> stone hopes praying with upcast eyes, old Ireland's
> hearts and hands.[6]

Here Bloom's mind has transformed reality into an immense
graveyard of all his expectations of life. What life seemed to
promise him is dead. The frustration is intensively expressed
in the short and broken sentences that he says to himself.

Poe achieved similar effects in "Loss of Breath" when the narrator loses the powers of speech after his operation, or in
"Berenice" when the menial speaks in broken sentences with wild
terrified looks.

Joyce's and Poe's protagonists often live in a deliberately culti-
vated isolation from their human environment and experience
frustrations from their fragmented forms of life. Each of the
stories in "Dubliners" dissects limited sections of Dublin society,
suggesting their political, social, or religious decay. The characters live isolated from one another, since they are either deaf,
blind or silent. The Poesque characters of "The Sisters" form
fragmentary parts of a society, as do the broken parts of the
priest's chalice; yet in their fragmentary condition they still hold
the forms of community or chalice together in a unity. In a
similar way, Poe shows how beyond the broken appearance of
parts, a perfect adaptation of these parts to each other exists.
Poe contrasts this spatial adaptation of parts to parts with the
crumbling condition of individual stones in "The Fall of the
House of Usher": "No portion of the masonry had fallen; and

there appeared to be a wild inconsistency between its still perfect adaptation of parts, and the crumbling condition of the individual stones."[7]

In "The Gold-Bug" Poe had suggested a similar image of fragmentation: "These stones had all been broken up from their settings and thrown loose in the chest."[8] These dislocated fragments stimulate the protagonists to decipher their relationships to one another. After having revealed the relationship of these broken elements, another reality unfolds:

> In scrutinizing the edges of the paper, I observed them to be more *chafed* than seemed necessary. They presented the *broken* appearance which is manifested when a stiff paper, having been once folded and pressed with a folder, is refolded in a reversed direction, in the same creases or edges which had formed the original fold. This discovery was sufficient. It was clear to me that the letter had been turned, as a glove, inside out, redirected and re-sealed.[9]

In a very similar way, Stephen's search for an absolute beyond reality is satisfied when he falls asleep and views the cyclic movement of the earth from her inside:

> His soul was swooning into some new world, fantastic, dim, uncertain as under sea, traversed by cloudy shapes and beings. A world, a glimmer, or a flower? Glimmering and trembling, trembling and unfolding, a breaking light, an opening flower, it spread in endless succession to itself, breaking in full crimson and unfolding and fading to palest rose, leaf by leaf and wave of light by wave of light, flooding all the heavens with its soft flushes, every flush deeper than the other.[10]

Poe and Joyce decipher reality by scrutinizing the essence of the fragments that they encounter.

The narrator of "The Pit and the Pendulum" is able to reorientate himself with the help of a fragment of his robe and some minute crevice of the masonry, from which he figures out that his enclosure has many irregularities and angles, yet that its general shape is that of a square with a circular pit in the middle.[11] This mental reconstruction of reality Joyce shows in "The Boarding House" when Mrs. Mooney makes Mary collect "the crusts and pieces" of broken bread. She begins then "to reconstruct" an interview.[12] Similarly for Stephen, after

> the stars began to crumble and a cloud of fine stardust fell through space . . . another equation began to unfold itself slowly and to spread abroad its widening tail. It was his own soul going forth to experience, unfolding itself sin by sin, spreading abroad the balefire of its burning stars and folding back upon itself, fading slowly, quenching its own lights and fires. They were quenched: and the cold darkness filled chaos.[13]

Stephen recognizes his own identity by deciphering the crumbling of the stars. Like these stars, fissures and cracks also are physical extensions of the protagonist's states of mind. The fissure in zigzag direction in the walls of Usher's rotten mansion indicates his character's split into rational and irrational qualities. When Madeline, Usher's other self, is struggling to get out of her coffin, her exertions find physical expression in the luminous effusion from the fissure about the entire building.

This split of rational and irrational orders is symbolized in the fissure in "A Portrait of the Artist," imaging Stephen's break with the church; the effusion of light from the fissure parallels his hallucinations of madness:

> The chapel was flooded by the dull scarlet light that filtered through the lowered blinds; and through the fissure between the last blind and the sash a shaft of wan light entered like a spear and touched the embossed brasses of the candlesticks upon the altar that gleamed like the battleworn mail armour of angels.[14]

The image of the fissure or crack foreshadows the material or spiritual dissolution of the protagonist. As the fissure in the walls of the house of Usher predicts the collapse of the mansions and

Usher in an effusion of light, similarly Stephen, being punished for having broken his glasses, experiences the crack of the whip forever.

When the border between the rational and irrational world order dissolves, Poe's and Joyce's protagonists peer through a murky and wavering grey twilight of looming, muttering figures which are confused with each other. This group of images in Poe's "The Spectacles" and Joyce's "A Portrait of the Artist" is intensified by the weakness of the protagonist's eyes. The narrator of "The Spectacles" perceives gestures and forms of a woman, an incarnation of ideal beauty, with whom he engages in "long, earnest, uninterrupted" conversations.[15] This weaving of bright poetic images with fragmentary abstractions is an expression of the way Stephen in *Ulysses* perceives reality. In the fleeting movement of forms a new concept of time and space is involved.

This fragmentation of images is in Poe's and Joyce's aesthetics an essential procedure in order to transmute the crude matter of the external world according to their soul's expression. They break this crude matter up into fragmentary parts and rearrange it. This technique does not imply any moral or didactic values which Poe and Joyce disregard for this reason. They are aware, however, of the necessity to rearrange the linguistic means anew.

To Stephen the method of dissecting crude matter of fact and of rearranging the fragments is a way of conceiving his reality:

> At night he built up on the parlour table an image of the wonderful island cave out of transfers and paper flowers and coloured tissue paper and strips of the silver and golden paper in which chocolate is wrapped. When he had broken up this scenery, weary of its tinsel, there would come to his mind the bright picture of Marseilles, of sunny trellises and of Mercedes.[16]

The method of dissecting and rearranging an image is a constructive procedure and Stephen refers to it as a vivisection.[17] This method of vivisection, adapted from Poe, is fully realized in *Ulysses*, where Joyce places man in an intense field of reference, giving fragmentary glimpses of history, geography, of the ascent and descent of mankind. All these fragmentary glimpses are presented according to a logical plan. Thus Stephen tries to reconstruct some fragments of Shakespeare and to declare them as fragments of a large literary tradition and to melt these fragments with his life to an inseparable unity. These fragmented elements in Poe's and Joyce's imagery are fitted in symmetrical relations to one another; any term of them, with equal appropriateness, is cause and effect. "Gradually," as Stephen's soul is "enriched with spiritual knowledge, he [sees] the whole world forming one vast symmetrical expression of God's power and love."[18] Similarly, Poe had argued in "Eureka" that our propensity for the symmetrical is the poetical essence of the universe. Consequently, Poe and Joyce poetize nature by imposing on it a certain symmetricality. The process of reconstruction from discordant fragments is a godlike act. Stephen formulates this creative act in *Ulysses*. "He [Stephen] affirmed his significance . . . as a conscious rational reagent between a micro- and a macrocosm ineluctably constructed upon the incertitude of the void."[19]

Like Poe, Joyce also endeavors to create literature with an architectural rather than organic structure. The structure is fragmentary in both Poe's and Joyce's work. They sacrifice organic and natural forms for an artificial form of fragmentation. Poe lists clues, Joyce epiphanies, from which both writers arrange the required associations for a perfect form of art.

Circular Imagery

Poe and Joyce create a labyrinth of consciousness. The errings of the souls of their protagonists are externalized in the images of winding staircases, corridors, boxes, castles, remote towers and turret rooms. With this imagery they express the night of their conscience and penetrate to the deepest recesses of their mental experiences. These mental experiences are in the most frequent instances externalized in images of circles and cycles.

Poe and Joyce find in the circle an order that is not limited to any given time or place. Each particular microscopic circle is related to ever larger circles that expand in the "general" universe and relate finally all existence to the cycles of the macrocosmos. This expansion of the particular circle into general cycles transforms the particular geographic locations into a Supreme Everywhere, and transforms the individual character into Everyman who lives, independent of time and space. Poe and Joyce totalize in this way the view of an object, of man, of nature by the expanding tendency of the circle into cycles.

This expanding cycle in Joyce's and Poe's work creates a new sense of time and space. Both writers displace time and place entirely, so that there exists only the recognition of nothingness. In "The Colloquy of Monos and Una" the standard senses are replaced by that of duration. Time ceases to have any measurable validity and becomes a universal absolute. "The absolute equalization" of time emerges into the "cycles of the firmamental orbs themselves."[20] Parallel with this equalization of time runs Monos' transformation. He passes through the physical, intellectual and spiritual being by which his body dissolves into nothingness. Joyce in his work shows a similar development: at the end of "Dubliners" time and location are displaced:

> The blinds would be drawn down . . . they were all becoming shades. . . . His [Gabriel's] soul had approached that region where dwell the vast hosts of the dead. He was conscious of, but could not apprehend their wayward and flickering existence. His own identity was fading out into a grey impalpable world: the solid world itself, which these dead had one time reared and lived in, was dissolving and dwindling.[21]

From this dissolution into nothingness the circle of life accomplishes a new stage, the stage of rebirth and metamorphosis. Monos says that man, as a race, should not become extinct, but be born again. Monos discusses with Una the rebirth into afterlife. This theme becomes in Joyce's "A Portrait of the Artist" a central image around which the cycles of life take form and transform themselves until Stephen realizes in *Ulysses* that a stone becomes a plant, a plant an animal, an animal a man, a man a spirit, and a spirit a God.

Poe explains in "Eureka" the theoretical evolution from the microcosmic circle to the macrocosmic cycle, discussing how from a single, unified primordial particle, brought into being by God, divided and radiated by Him into a limited area of infinite space, a finite number of atoms revert back toward the center. Impelled by the desire for unity (attraction, gravitation) though restrained from absolute union among themselves (repulsion, electricity) they finally realize the greatest possible quantitative as well as qualitative complexity (which was the purpose of their diffusion). The repulsive force, giving way before the collective tendency, subsides into the original one, or unity. Poe inferred the law of the dissipation of energy from Newton that suggests that all things in the world push toward some ineffable common center; they struggle back to this One that for Poe became the general center of irradiation. Poe approaches his concluding conception, namely that man becomes God, by affirming that the same process of "creation" and irradiation, returning into itself, will happen again and again: "a novel universe, swelling into existence and then subsiding into nothingness, at every throb of the heart divine. This heart divine," Poe says, "is our own."[22] Further, Poe formulated in "The Island of the Fay" the expanding tendency from circle to circle:

> As we find cycle within cycle without end,—yet all revolving around one far-distant centre which is the Godhead, may we not analogically suppose in the same manner, life within life, the less within the greater, and all within the Spirit Divine?[23]

Poe's theory is closely related to what Joyce realized in his work. In regard to this cyclic movement toward Godhead, Daedalus asserts in the Library scene in *Ulysses* that "All is All," that everything is in a sense everything else. William York Tindall, referring in particular to "A Portrait of the Artist," compares the method to that of "masses of material held in balance like the solar system by attraction and repulsion. It is this balance in a work of art that Stephen calls static."[24] This static center is Dublin, which is always the center in Joyce's work. Dublin is a center for "Dubliners," it is a labyrinth for Daedalus, the mediterranean sea for *Ulysses*, and it expands finally into the nebulous universe of *Finnegans Wake*. Thus the expansion from a microcosmic center into the universe in all directions takes the form of a cyclic diffusion, according to a principle similar to Poe's law of irradiation.

In "Dubliners" there is a motion from a dark central room, in the North, toward the world of wild sensations in the west, and it ends by the universal plain in which not the individual existence but existence in general is of importance. It is not the unique event that counts but whatever is general, and this embraces more than individual small identity to include all the people alive and dead. The general idea of the dead is expressed by the image of snow that falls all over Ireland and which closes a cycle around the island. Hence, the motion of "Dubliners" starts from a small center and spreads then in enlarging cycles all over Ireland and into the whole universe. From there the motion of return to the center starts with "A Portrait of the Artist." Stephen walks from one geographic and spiritual orbit to another. The cyclic movement is directed from an outside toward an interior center. At the beginning Stephen is twenty miles from the city, in Clongowes College. Monuments, itineraries, distances are very precisely denoted. Stephen tries to place himself in the universe and to find out how he is related to that "big ball in the middle of the clouds."[25] He finds out that he himself is a small center around which expands the "class of elements," the Clongowes Wood College, Sallins, County Kildare, Ireland, Europe, The World, The Universe—and finally the question arises: "What was after the universe?"[26] As Stephen walks on, all the topographical denotations lose their precision steadily and the city interiorizes. He sets forth on a lengthening radius to the "dappled and seaborne"[27] clouds that float beyond Ireland and all over Europe. Stephen is ready to take flight and find out what comes after the universe.

Stephen's interior life and the moral conflict of the artist become that of man in general in *Ulysses*. Each myth that Joyce depicts in this novel of one single day, June 16, 1904, in Dublin, has significance in the individual structure of a definite life. Yet it points at the same time beyond this single life into a timeless and spaceless sphere of man's inner life. It is common to all experiences of man that the most banal things become cosmic events. Joyce depicts the recurrence of these events in *Ulysses*. The essential traits of the most banal desires and purest dreams of the artist are complemented by a long and monotonous soliloquy of the woman in bed, whose heartbeat joins the rhythmical movement of earth and that of the sensible universe. This type of analogy between trivial things and cosmic events Poe expresses in "Ligeia":

> I found, in the commonest objects of the universe, a circle of analogies to that expression. I mean to say that, subsequently to the period when Ligeia's beauty passed into my spirit, there dwelling as in a shrine, I derived, from many existences in the material world, a sentiment such as I felt always around, within me, by her large and luminous orbs. Yet not the more could I define that sentiment, or analyze, or even steadily view it. I recognized it, let me repeat, sometimes in the survey of a rapidly growing vine—in the contemplation of a moth, a butterfly, a chrysalis, a stream of running water. I have felt it in the ocean in the falling of a meteor.[28]

The expansion from particulars into generalities is achieved in the widest and completest sense in *Finnegans Wake*. With *Finnegans Wake* Dublin becomes the universal city freed from all geographical and temporal boundaries.

As we have noticed, with the end of "The Dead" Dublin is a general location in the universe. Stephen, in "A Portrait of the Artist," considers all the spiritual conflicts of his youth in relation to the universe; these individual emotions are transformed into universal ones in *Ulysses*. Joyce shows that even the banal world has its relation to spirituality. With *Finnegans Wake* Dublin becomes the city of cities, the Liffey the river of all rivers and the heights of Nowth rise as world mountains. Poe's and Joyce's circular imagery reveals that the circle expands from all objects to the remotest spheres and from these spheres it again diminishes. Poe formulates this theory of cyclic evolution in "Eureka": "the cycles of the Universe are perpetual—the Universe has no conceivable end."[29] Only the artist has the "Divine capacity to adapt the end." This end Poe formulated as the highest kind of poetic insight:

> . . . the symmetry of principle sees the end of all things metaphysically involved in the thought of a beginning; seeks and finds, in this origin of all things the *rudiment* of this end; and perceives the impiety of supposing this end likely to be brought about less simply,—less directly, —less obviously,—less artistically,—than through the *reaction of the originating Act*.[30]

This reaction of the originating act involves the idea that the universe is an extension and a symbolization of God.

Poe and Joyce express the beginning and end of all things in the following groups of circular images:

1. Circle within circle.
2. Circular images that express a motion toward the center.
3. Static images of the center.
4. Imagery of departure and return.
5. Imagery of circular imprisonment.

Circle within Circle

The imagery of the circle as an expanding form relates objects with man and cosmos in many images of Poe. In "The Spectacles" the narrator observes that the lady's "admirable roundness of the wrist was well set off by the bracelet which encircled it."[31] The saucer eyes of the Dutch burghers in "The Devil in the Belfry" are paralleled by the "perfect circular valley,"[32] around which "extends a range of mountains" (as in "Eleanora") and a "continuous row of sixty little houses, looking toward the center of the plain";[33] there are circular paths as round as the sundial; in symmetrical order twenty-four cabbages of round form grow, indicating symbolically the twenty-four hours of the day. In "A Descent into the Maelstrom" there are two circular islands surrounded by the gulf and the semicircle of the shore line. The mountains are surrounded by a belt of vapor; the "circular rift of clear sky"[34] opens in contrast to the blackness of the pool's center. In that rift appears the full moon, again an image of roundness.

These circular images relate objects, man, and nature by wavelike expansion, starting sometimes from several centers within the same story, in Joyce's "Dubliners." In "Two Gallants," while Corley and Lenehan take their walk through the city, while memories "of summer, circulated in the streets,"[35] the wavelike expression of their narratives is followed by bursts of wheezing laughter. The two gallants look at a three-dimensional and sometimes a two-dimensional sphere. "Lenehan's gaze was fixed on the large faint moon circled with a double halo. . . . Corley gazed at the pale disc of the moon, now nearly veiled."[36] They meet a woman, executing half turns on her heels, and the "silver buckle of her belt seemed to depress the centre of her body" that is as round as a ball, being short, stout and muscular.[37] Lenehan watched Corley's head which "turned at every moment towards the young woman's face like a big ball revolving on a pivot."[38] Lenehan enters a restaurant and sees a "segment" of plum pudding. The circular image finds final expression in a small gold coin at the end of the story.

Circular Images that Express a Motion toward the Center

Poe's and Joyce's images illustrate that the movement downward usually leads in ever faster velocity into a bottomless abyss of destruction. Poe and Joyce use many similar images connoting this circular motion: funnel, vortex, tunnel, whirlpool, moskoe or maelstrom, adjectives and nouns such as giddy, dizzy, round and round, revolving, circuit, circumference, cube, barrel, embrace, enveloped, unfolding, cylindrical, surrounded.[39]

The circular image inheres in the round forms of nature that Stephen observes in the ideal Poe-like landscape garden: when Stephen climbs to the crest of a sandhill, he gazes about him and discovers that

> a rim of the young moon cleft the pale waste of skyline, the rim of a silver hoop embedded in grey sand; and the tide was flowing in fast to the land with a low whisper of her waves, islanding a few last figures in distant pools.[40]

Finally, Stephen looks into "the dark pool of a jar."[41] It is significant that this motion is directed from a large to ever smaller circles, sustained by the fast movement of the waves. The yellow dripping of tea which makes a dark pool and is "scooped out like a boghole,"[42] reminds Stephen of the turf-colored water of the bath in Clongowes. The image of turf-colored water recalls Usher's deep and dark tarn that closes sullenly and silently over the fragments of the House of Usher.

If we consider "A Portrait of the Artist" as a whole, then this ever faster cyclic movement toward the center of all-absorbing life is well expressed with the progressing stages to Stephen's maturity. At first Stephen only timidly circles around the neighboring square:[43] many voices urge him toward a movement of national revival. Steadily the faces he knew fall asunder while he runs in ever faster steps up and then down the hill.[44] Stephen observes how dense and maddening fumes rise and pass away above him till at last the air is clear and cold, a parallel image to the pure white idealized streams and lakes in "Eleanora" and "Landor's Cottage." Stephen observes the sky and clouds in "a fantastic world of sombre masses with lakelike spaces of dark rosy light."[45] These images of lakelike spaces deepen. "An abyss of fortune or of temperament sundered him from them (his parents) . . . he was drifting amid life like the barren shell of the moon," remembering Shelley's lines how "the alternation of sad human ineffectiveness with vast inhuman cycles of activity chilled him."[46] After this static emotion, comparable to Pym's last vision of the passive grey face at the end of the story, the chapter ends with the static circular image of Stephen, standing still in the middle of the room, when "she came over to him and embraced him gaily and gravely with her round arms."[47] The circles enclose Stephen in ever narrower space, where goatish creatures "moved in slow circles, circling closer and closer to enclose, to enclose, soft language issuing from their lips, their long swishing tails besmeared with stale shite, thrusting upwards their terrific faces . . . Help!"[48] The climax of this life-absorbing circular motion is reached at the end of "A Portrait of the Artist," when Stephen is invited to new experiences: there are strange diversities all of which on the periphery of Stephen's experiences would be gathered into a center of himself, his being.

> April 16. Away! Away! The spell of arms and voices: the white arms of roads, their promise of close embraces and the black arms of tall ships that stand against the moon, their tale of distant nations. They are held out to say: We are alone—come. And the voices say with them: We are your kinsmen. And the air is thick with their company as they call to me, their kinsmen, making ready to go, shaking the wings of their exultant and terrible youth.[49]

This quest for imaginary voyages is in Poe's stories a catastrophic urge, since knowledge is attained, as the circular images of whirlpools, abysses and life-absorbing waters illustrate, only at the price of destruction.

The eagerness to confront the unknown is in Poe's imagery extended to the brink of the abyss, in Joyce's imagery to the slope of a river.[50] The ends of "Eveline" and "Narrative of A. Gordon Pym" depict the protagonists hurrying onward to some exciting knowledge whose attainment is destruction, by the loss of the protagonists' identity, as it is symbolically expressed in their white, passive-looking faces.

In contrast to Poe's frequent circular images of self-destruction ("A Descent into the Maelstrom," "MS. Found in a Bottle," "Narrative of A. Gordon Pym," "William Wilson"), Stephen in

"Portrait of the Artist" never achieves self-destruction; although close to falling into the abyss, he comes up to the crest again, since "the chaos in which his ardour extinguished itself was a cold indifferent knowledge of himself"[51] and then "what did it avail to pray, when he knew that his soul lusted after its own destruction?"[52] Even in *Ulysses*, after Stephen has paid for the damage he has done to a chandelier, Bloom tries to keep Stephen from a quarrel with English soldiers: "The midnight sun is darkened. The earth trembles . . . a chasm opens with a noiseless yawn." Stephen is struck by one of his soldiers, "totters, collapses, falls stunned,"[53] but he revives and Bloom takes him to his home. This image shows that although Stephen totters to his center, he does not seek ultimate knowledge in self-destruction, as did Poe's protagonists.

Static Images of the Center

Poe and Joyce arrest the action in states of extreme emotions by focusing on the static image of the "middle." Poe expresses states of enchantment in "Tamerlane," by referring continually to the summer of his youth. He pronounces the daydream "Fearfully beautiful! the real nothing of midday waking life," and he admires the "noon-day beauty—which is all."[54] This enchantment is carried on in "The Assignation" when Aphrodite appears at midnight in midsummer; in "Eleanora" the enchantment comes from nature, from fantastic trees that fall into the center of the valley; in "The Island of the Fay" a small circular island lies in the center of the valley; uncommon visions issue from the central point in "The Pit and the Pendulum." In "Ligeia" a mysterious type of horror is attached to Lady Rowena whose advancement to the middle of the room chills her husband into stone. Horror is suggested by images of waters that fall into abysses without bottom in "The Unparalleled Adventures of One Hans Pfaall" or in the bottomless vales of "Dreamland"; masquerades suggest horror, for example, when in "Hop-Frog" the King and his seven friends find themselves in the center of the room and Hop-Frog scrambles over the heads of the crowd to the wall and then returns to the center of the room.

As in Poe's work, images of the center, in enchantment or horror, are points of arrest in Joyce's imagery. When Stephen "stood still in the middle of the roadway," his heart was "clamouring against his bosom in a tumult";[55]

> He was alone. He was unheeded, happy, and near to the wild heart of life. He was alone and young and wilful and wildhearted, alone amid a waste of wild air and brackish waters and the seaharvest of shells and tangle and veiled grey sunlight and gayclad figures of children and girls and voices childish and girlish in the air.
> A girl stood before him in midstream, alone and still, gazing out to sea. She seemed like one whom magic had changed into the likeness of a strange and beautiful seabird.[56]

Similarly to this beauty in midstream, Stephen sees the "Blessed Virgin . . . in the middle of a hamshaped encampment of poor cottages";[57] and "as he stood still in the middle of the room she came over to him and embraced him gaily and gravely."[58]

Poe's and Joyce's protagonists very often direct their eyes toward the center of the plain: the houses and their owner in "The Devil in the Belfry" by Poe concentrate on a central point. There the devil with his circular eye evaporates into smoke. The eyes are fixed on dominant figures of horror and strangeness in "The Man of the Crowd" and in "An Encounter."

Sometimes a center is the point of departure for wild adventures, as it is the central apple tree in "Araby," by Joyce, a center that is counterbalanced by the center of the big hall of Stephen's imagination at the end of his trip.

There is a basic difference in Poe's and Joyce's imagery of departure and return, since Poe's protagonists if once carried away in cyclic motions toward the center do not return again, whereas Stephen frees himself with as much skill as Bloom in *Ulysses.*

Imagery of Departure and Return

There is a path that leads to the innermost life, and in seeking to apprehend its direction, we may think of it as both a return and an advance. This type of imagery we find in Poe's "The Island of the Fay." The fay, living on a circular island and circling in ever-closer circles around the island, reappears in summer and winter and finally disappears in the darkness of the "region of ebony flood." In "The Domain of Arnheim" by Poe, the mysterious departures and returns of a traveler make him lose his sense of direction. In "Ms. Found in a Bottle" the protagonists are whirling dizzily in immense concentric circles. All these winding circles absorb the protagonists. However, their departures and returns are balanced by new centers from which the circling movement starts anew.

In Joyce's "An Encounter" the stranger steps out at a distant end of the field and returns; and while Stephen looks at the foot of the slope, the stranger's mind circles around the same orbit. Then he steps out again, and in returning his mind has found "a new center" of repeating a common subject again and again. In *Ulysses* the theme reinforces in larger proportions the idea of the cycle. The "Aeolus" chapter begins before Nelson's pillar when a starter is sending off trams into various directions; we then follow Bloom as he enters Aeolus' home, the office of the *Evening Telegraph*. Bloom hurries off in pursuit of an advertisement. Near the end of the chapter Bloom returns and we see trams standing in their tracks, bound for many directions. The chapter ends before Nelson's pillar.[59]

Another theme of departure and return is stressed in *Ulysses* when Bloom recalls the way his friend walked. "On the South Circular road in the company of Elsa Potter, followed by an individual of sinister aspect, she [Milly] went half way down Stamer street and turned abruptly back (reason of change not stated)."[60] Then Bloom discovers the temporary departure of his cat that recalls a similar departure of the cat in "An Encounter." These mysterious departures and returns seem to be steady advances in an attempt to find out where the universe ends.

This movement of return and departure is also of symbolic significance in nature imagery. In "The Domain of Arnheim" by Poe, the river opens from time to time to form lakes. Similarly the rivers in "A Portrait of the Artist" open at the strand and invite the protagonists to new experiences of wild sensations. Ellison dreams of a "new race of fairies" and fancies "a panoramic cataract of rubies, sapphires, opals, and golden onyxes, rolling silently out of the sky."[61] Stephen's

> soul was swooning into some new world, fantastic, dim, uncertain as under sea, traversed by cloudy shapes and beings. A world, a glimmer, or a flower? Glimmering and trembling, trembling and unfolding, a breaking light, an opening flower, it spread in endless succession to itself, breaking in full crimson and unfolding and fading to palest rose, leaf by leaf and wave of light by wave of light, flooding all the heavens with its soft flushes, every flush deeper than the other.[62]

Thus in Poe and Joyce the image of a departing river that expands and loses itself in a larger water invites Ellison and Stephen to live the visions of a world of dreams and fancies.

Imagery of Circular Imprisonment

Fog and mist are circular images of enclosure in both Poe's and Joyce's work. In "Dreamland" and "Fairy-Land" there is a veil of mist over the dim or bottomless valley and on the shadowy and boundless floods respectively. Grey mist in Poe's and Joyce's imagery is a characteristic component of states between dreaming and waking, between unreality and reality. In "Eveline," for example, mist is the symbol that separates these two worlds, when the "boat blew its mournful whistle into the mist."[63]

The prevailing images of the narrow, labyrinthine streets, through which Stephen, Pym, or the protagonist in "Man of the Crowd" pass are those of rain, of fog, and of smoke-clogged air. Not only do the nightly wanderings of these protagonists through fog and mist turn moister with each turn downward, but mist penetrates also the hearts of the people of Dublin, since they are all dull, austere, and colorless like dust. They are all portrayed as stern, humorless, urban dwellers. The grey mist all over Ireland has an evilly portentous parallel to the images of dim mist all over the earth[64] at the death of Morella or to the reference to "the wan and the misty-winged Ashtophet of idolatrous Egypt" that presides over "marriages ill-omened" in "Ligeia."[65]

Sometimes fog and mist become heavy and suffocating, hanging threateningly upon the protagonists; this dead weight of mist and dust relates Poe's "Shadow—A Parable" and Joyce's "The Dead" as Levin points out.[66] Similarly, Usher and Madeline live "in the gradual yet certain condensation of an atmosphere of their own about the waters and the walls."[67] This image shows the expansion of the circular image of mist into an ever thicker atmosphere, and finally it becomes a wall that encircles the protagonists in a circular imprisonment.

These images of circular imprisonment illustrate that for Poe and Joyce nothing exists beyond the psychic limits within which the realities become dreams, such as Berenice formulates. Wilson questions this mental universe: "Am I not now dying a victim to the horror and the mystery of the wildest of all sublunary visions?"[68] Stephen is able to free himself from those circling visions of goatish creatures that seem to strangle him. He observes:

> The rain had drawn off; and amid the moving vapours from point to point of light the city was spinning about herself a soft cocoon of yellowish haze. Heaven was still and faintly luminous.[69]

Poe and Joyce show the growing realm of the subconscious in the image of the labyrinth; Pym and Stephen creep through innumerable gloomy and winding narrow passages in order to reach an iron-bound box or the director's castle. To Pym and Stephen these winding staircases and galleries are their symbolic prison of existence. All these images of staircases, boxes, and the like are the pictorial and frenzied manifestations of Pym's and Stephen's mind. These states of mind become in *Ulysses* a labyrinthine art form in the structure of the interior monologue.

The images of mental captivity have sometimes a maddening

effect upon the protagonist. The circular dungeon, the circular pit in "The Pit and the Pendulum," the round eyes in the steel walls put the narrator in a state of madness. Similarly, the stranger in "An Encounter" is a captive of his own condition, since his mind is circling round and round the same orbit, like that of the prisoner in the circular pit. Gabriel Conroy, in "The Dead" suffers the same circular mental irritation, since repeatedly he "began to rub the knuckles of his left fist backwards and forwards into his left eye,"[70] repeating the same words over and over again.

Besides these images of mental imprisonment, Poe's and Joyce's circular images of captivity show further affinities in the images of physical imprisonment that make the protagonists unable to change their living conditions. Circular valleys ("Eleanora"), palaces ("The Fall of the House of Usher," "Berenice"), castellated abbeys ("The Masque of the Red Death"), walls of water, ramparts of ice ("Ms. Found in a Bottle," "The Descent into the Maelstrom"), continuous walls of the universe ("The Power of Words"), prison-like ramparts ("William Wilson"), are paralleled by Joyce's images of the walls of the universe ("Dubliners"), vaulted halls ("Araby"), circumpolar icecaps (*Ulysses*),[71] and the circular roads around Dublin.

All these images of circular imprisonment, whether mental or physical, illustrate that Poe's and Joyce's protagonists live in their own time and space, independently and cut off from the world outside, for the world outside exists for Poe and Joyce in complete subservience to the will of thought. The protagonists become prisoners of the orbits of their own minds. The circular image relates microcosmos with macrocosmos.

Poe's and Joyce's protagonists find, as all imaginary travelers, at the end of their passage into the depths of a labyrinth, a metamorphosis of their ego. This metamorphosis Marcel Brion describes:

> Pour le voyageur qui pénètre dans le labyrinthe, le but est d'atteindre la chambre centrale, la crypte des mystères. Mais lorsqu'il l'a atteinte, il doit en sortir et regagner le monde extérieur, parvenir en somme à une

nouvelle naissance: tel est le contenu de toutes les religions de mystères, et de toutes les sectes qui regardent le voyage dans le labyrinthe comme le processus nécessaire des métamorphoses d'où surgit un homme nouveau. Plus le voyage est difficile, plus les obstacles sont nombreux et ardus, plus l'adepte se transforme et, au cours de cette initiation itinérante, acquiert un nouveau moi.[72]

Thus the travels without horizon through a labyrinth of possible passages lead the travelers in Poe's and Joyce's work to ever higher stages of maturity.

In summary, Poe's and Joyce's protagonists perceive the world that surrounds them, on the one hand, broken up into a series of detached aspects, and on the other hand, regrouped into images of geometrical order and form.

CHAPTER THREE

The Imagery of the Setting

Poe and Joyce reflect in their imagery a great concern for
form, since form is to them a product of the imagination. Their
devices for the achievement of symbolic form become apparent
in an examination of their treatment of the physical elements in
nature and the artifacts of its inhabitants. These represent habits
of the writers' imagination and thought. They construct anew
the shapes, sizes, and features of the world of appearances. The
aim of both writers is not to describe the world they see but to
evoke essences of it in the reader's imagination. Joyce says himself that he is the priest of the eternal imagination, transmuting
the daily bread of experience into the radiant body of ever living
life.[1] Thus the aesthetic image expresses the essence of things
beautiful.[2]

Discovering this essence of beautiful things consists for Poe
and Joyce in making their environment an analogous image to
the structure of their mind. Thus for them a tree, understood in
its artistic context as a vegetable form, would be dead if their
imagination did not make it live as an image. And this image is
to them true life. This reality is revealed in signatures that the
two writers discover in nature, the creation of an objective world.
Poe in "Al Aaraaf" recognizes that nature speaks a mysterious
language of half-hidden meanings. "All nature speaks, and ev'n
ideal things Flap shadowy sounds from visionary wings."[3] The
theory, an extension of the Platonic system of ideas, has a touch
of mysticism. This mysticism attracts Stephen and Bloom:
Stephen, asking himself one morning on the beach what reality
is, states:

> Signatures of all things I am here to read, sea-spawn
> and seawrack, the nearing tide, that rusty boot. Snot-
> green, bluesilver, rust-coloured signs. Limits of the
> diaphane.[4]

Poe and Joyce, as these images illustrate, try to read the essences of the visible universe. This universe, as the similar perceptions of Stephen and Bloom prove, is present in their minds.
They are able to conceive what lies beyond that reality, the truth
or essence of all things.

These realities are for Poe and Joyce not only revealed in
nature but also in furniture. Both Poe and Joyce pay great attention to furniture. Furniture is the physical extension of their
protagonists' own spirit. The protagonist imposes his subjective
order of mind on the order in the world outside: thus the vegetable and material world partakes and reflects the psychical and
mental life of the protagonists. This order is best preserved when
they do not have any interest in other people. They live in isolation as Shem did in

> The house O'Shea or O'Shame, *Quivapieno*, known as
> the Haunted Inkbottle, no number Brimstone Walk,
> Asia in Ireland, as it was infested with raps, with his
> penname SHUT sepiascraped on the doorplate and a
> blind of black sailcloth over its wan phwinshogue, in
> which the soul-contracted son of the secret cell groped
> through life. . . .[5]

After giving a catalogue of Shem's "literary furniture," speaking of "distortions, inversions of all this chambermade music,"
the protagonist feels

> self exiled in upon his ego, a nightlong a shaking be-
> twixtween white or reddr hawrors, noondayterrorised
> to skin and bone by an ineluctable phantom (may the
> Shaper have mercery on him!) writing the mystery of
> himsel in furniture.[6]

The above description of O'Shea's house shows how confined are the quarters in which Joyce's protagonist lives. This confinement is an aesthetic device, associating incident and its enclosing frame, the life of the protagonist with his closest environment. Poe, in "The Philosophy of Composition," urges that "a close *circumscription of space* is necessary to the insulated incident." Such a setting, he points out, "has the force of a frame to a picture."[7] The association of frame and picture leads Joyce to the confinement of a location by a frame, the material of which stands in close relationship to the location: Joyce, in his talk to Frank O'Connor,

> calling on him in Paris noticed a picture of Cork in a very odd frame. "Yes," said Joyce, "I had the greatest difficulty in getting that frame, but naturally a view of Cork could only be framed in Cork."[8]

This analogy of frame and location has nothing to do with unity of place. It is for Poe and Joyce a point of departure into a world of wild sensations.

The order in which the materials of this chapter will appear is as follows. The picture frame of which Poe and Joyce speak is a proscenium to a stage. For this reason I treat first the setting of the stage, then the relationship of forms in nature, of furniture, and of men to each other. Further, I illustrate the isolated position of the protagonists and its effect on their imagination; and finally I shall try to relate the stage lighting in Poe's work to that in Joyce's.

The Setting of the Stage

All forms have to be related to each other. Poe emphasizes in "Landor's Cottage" that the arrangement of geometrical forms of furniture is to be strictly observed. It impresses the onlooker in a certain way.

> On the floor was an ingrain carpet, of excellent texture —a white ground, spotted with small circular green figures. At the windows were curtains of snowy white

jaconet muslin: they were tolerably full, and hung *decisively*, perhaps rather formally, in sharp, parallel plaits to the floor—*just* to the floor. The walls were papered with a French paper of great delicacy, a silver ground, with a faint green cord running zig-zag throughout. Its expanse was relieved merely by three of Julien's exquisite lithographs *à trois crayons*, fastened to the wall without frames. One of these drawings was a scene of Oriental luxury, or rather voluptuousness another was a "carnival piece," spirited beyond compare; the third was a Greek female head—a face so divinely beautiful, and yet of an expression so provokingly indeterminate, never before arrested my attention.

The more substantial furniture consisted of a round table, a few chairs (including a large rocking-chair), and a sofa, or rather "settee": its material was plain maple painted a creamy white, slightly interstriped with green—the seat of cane. The chairs and table were "to match;" but the *forms* of all had evidently been designed by the same brain which planned "the grounds": it is impossible to conceive anything more graceful.

On the table were a few books; a large, square, crystal bottle of some novel perfume; a plain, ground glass *astral* (not solar) lamp, with an Italian shade; and a large vase of resplendently-blooming flowers. Flowers indeed of gorgeous colors and delicate odor formed the sole mere *decoration* of the apartment. The fire-place was nearly filled with a vase of brilliant geranium. On a triangular shelf in each angle of the room stood also a similar vase, varied only as to its lovely contents. One or two smaller bouquets adorned the mantel; and late violets clustered about the open windows.[9]

The preoccupation with the arrangement of furniture, as seen in this passage above, shows how Poe attempts to achieve a symmetrical juxtaposition of the geometrical forms. In the same impressionistic way Poe observes the arrangement of scenes. Usher reflects that

there *are* combinations of very simple natural objects
which have the power of affecting us . . . a mere different arrangement of the particulars of the scene, of the
details of the picture, would be sufficient to modify, or
perhaps to annihilate its capacity for sorrowful impression.[10]

This way of relating forms impressionistically to one another
is of central interest to Stephen in *Ulysses*. He gives to Bloom a
very exact inventory and at the same time a plan for the arrangement of the articles of furniture:

Describe the alterations effected in the disposition of
the articles of furnitures? . . . two chairs had been
moved from right and left of the ingleside to the position originally occupied by the blue and white checker
inlaid majolicatopped table.
Describe them.
One: a squat stuffed easychair with stout arms extended and back slanted to the rere, which, repelled in
recoil, had then upturned an irregular fringe of a rec-
tangular rug and now displayed on its amply unhol-
stered seat a centralised diffusing and diminishing dis-
colouration. The other: a slender splayfoot chair of
glossy cane curves, placed directly opposite the former,
its frame from top to seat and from seat to base being
varnished dark brown, its seat being a bright circle of
white plaited rush.
What significances attached to these two chairs?
Significance of similitude, of posture, of symbolism, of
circumstantial evidence, of testimonial supermanence.[11]

In this passage Joyce concentrates on forms, shapes, and sizes
of furniture. Joyce is putting curves, angles, circles, coils, squares,
angular and irregular forms about a center of diffusion that creates a symbolic relationship of these shaped forms with each
other. These geometrical forms and the impressionistic arrange-

ment of furniture Joyce observes also in stage-directions. Joyce sets the scene for "Exiles," in a form similar to Poe's conception in "Landor's Cottage."

> In the centre of the room a round table. Chairs, uphol-stered in faded green plush, stand round the table. To the right, forward, a smaller table with a smoking serv-ice on it. Near it an easychair and a lounge. Cocoanut mats lie before the fireplace, beside the lounge and be-fore the doors. The floor is of stained planking. The double doors at the back and the folding doors at the right have lace curtains, which are drawn halfway. The lower sash of the window is lifted and the window is hung with heavy green plush curtains. The blind is pulled down to the edge of the lifted lower sash. It is a warm afternoon in June and the room is filled with soft sunlight which is waning.[12]

These passages from Joyce's work show that he attempts to achieve a symmetrical juxtaposition of geometrical forms of furniture and at the same time to give the onlooker an impression as indefinite as that of impressionist painters.

The Relationship of Forms that Are Shaped in Squares and Circles

Joyce and Poe conceive persons as geometrical forms who move, as we have seen in the last chapter, in cycles, according to certain laws of attraction and repulsion. Besides this motion in circles and squares Poe and Joyce also strictly observe the relationship of persons to each other by their circular and angular shapes.

These squares and circles Poe observes in the contrast between the rounded, potbellied burghers and the thin, angular visitor of "The Devil in the Belfry." Another way of contrast Poe suggests in "The Pit and the Pendulum," where a dreamy, inde-terminate hum suggests revolution, "with the burr of a mill-wheel."[13] These circular images are contrasted by the vertical images of the judges with their thin, white lips; these judges, set in opposition to the victim, look to the victim like unmovable towers in comparison to his own mental vertigo. The horror rises from the huge pendulum with its semi-circular swing, striking the hours with a razor-like crescent in the circular abyss of the pit at right angles to the victim's length.

Clothing and grouping of persons are presented in contrasting forms in "Hop-Frog" by Poe. The king and ministers are encased in square-cut shirts and drawers. They attach themselves on a long chain in circular form.

These circular, angular and swinging forms Joyce combines in "Two Gallants." The swinging movement of the pendulum seems to be transferred to Corley's swaying of the head from side to side and the swinging movement of a lady's umbrella. The two gallants, Lenehan and Corley, come down the hill (this is a round form) to Rutland Square (angular image). The squat and ruddy Lenehan walks on the edge of the path, while Corley with his large and globular head moves like a pendulum. Lenehan describes an angle while walking across the street obliquely.

Joyce contrasts squares and circles in depicting two types of persons in the same way as Poe conceived them. In "Ivy Day in the Committee Room" he describes one person as a very fat man

> whose blue serge clothes seemed to be in danger of falling from his sloping figure. . . . The other man, who was much younger and frailer, had a thin, clean-shaven face. He wore a very high double collar and a wide-brimmed bowler hat.[14]

These two people have the shape of a cone and a cylinder.

As in "The Pit and the Pendulum," where circular images such as the burr of a mill wheel and the vertigo of the prisoners are contrasted with judges who look like towers, so there is a similar image in "A Portrait of the Artist as a Young Man," in the contrast of the image of wheeling with turret:

> . . . and he felt that the augury he had sought in the wheeling darting birds and in the pale space of sky above him had come forth from his heart like a bird from a turret quietly and swiftly.[15]

These round and angular forms relate also Joyce's objects of still life to each other:

> The green square of paper pinned round the lamp cast down a tender shade. On the dresser was a plate of sausages and white pudding and on the shelf there were eggs. . . . White pudding and eggs and cups of tea. How simple and beautiful was life after all![16]

All these images of squares and circles illustrate that there exists a close affinity between Poe's and Joyce's concepts of relating part to part, the form of inorganic squares and circles which are related to one another, to an organic whole.

Isolated Setting and Its Effect
on the Imagination

For Poe and Joyce, the exterior world, often *confined* to the landscape garden, a mansion, a backyard, lofty halls, rooms of different shapes with functional and decorative furniture, creates a certain atmosphere and the spiritual universe of the protagonists. Gothic windows, open or closed doors, improbable shadows on the floor, the vibrations of music, odors, and perfumes create a sequence of associations that stimulates the power of imagination of the protagonists to live in a world of wild sensations.

Only in complete isolation do the sensations of the protagonists come into play. Egaeus gives a very significant description of the way he contemplates the most ordinary objects of the universe:

> To muse for long unwearied hours, with my attention riveted to some frivolous device on the margin or in the typography of a book; to become absorbed, for the better part of a summer's day, in a quaint shadow falling aslant upon the tapestry or upon the floor; to lose myself, for an entire night, in watching the steady flame of a lamp, or the embers of a fire; to dream away whole days over the perfume of a flower; to repeat monot-

onously, some common word, until the sound, by dint
of frequent repetition, ceased to convey any idea whatever to the mind; to lose all sense of motion or physical
existence, by means of absolute bodily quiescence long
and obstinately persevered in: such were a few of the
most common and least pernicious vagaries induced by
a condition of the mental faculties, not, indeed, altogether unparalleled, but certainly bidding defiance to
any thing like analysis or explanation.[17]

Through the absolute negation of presence, sounds and motions, Poe's and Joyce's protagonists are driven like Egaeus into
self-isolation with an alter ego. In Joyce's "A Painful Case," Mr.
Duffy and Mrs. Sinico, withdrawn and cut off from the world
in a remote little cottage outside the city, spend moments of
mystic ecstasy:

The dark discreet room, their isolation, the music that
still vibrated in their ears united them. This union ex-
alted him, wore away the rough edges of his character,
emotionalised his mental life. Sometimes he caught himself listening to the sound of his own voice. He thought
that in her eyes he would ascend to an angelic stature;
and, as he attached the fervent nature of his companion
more and more closely to him, he heard the strange impersonal voice which he recognised as his own, insisting
on the soul's incurable loneliness. We cannot give ourselves, it said: we are our own. The end of these dis-
courses was that one night during which she had shown
every sign of unusual excitement, Mrs. Sinico caught up
his hand passionately and pressed it to her cheek.[18]

Duffy, like Egaeus in "Berenice" or Roderick in "Ligeia" is able
to live in complete understanding of the meaning of life, because
he is able to relate the elements of this world with the various
aspects of the transcendent entity that lies above and beyond.
This complete harmony is achieved because the emotions of the
protagonists are reflected in all the invisible essences that in-
vade the room: music, the lighting of the room, the atmosphere

of enclosure. These invisible elements are rigorously equivalent with their emotions and form a harmonious whole.

In "A Painful Case," as in "Ligeia," the issue is decided by the loss of identity: Roderick in "Ligeia" is unable to desire that she live, and her will is unable to survive. Being unable to share with Mrs. Sinico any longer his intellectual conversations, Mr. Duffy decides to live in complete isolation. Like the protagonist of Poe's "Silence" who is the "self" disgusted with the world of men and who seeks solitude, similarly Duffy wishes to withdraw in his ancient well-ordered room, the order of which still reflects the order of his state of mind at the time when he left it years ago. In self-isolation he loses his identity. He has lost his alter ego in Mrs. Sinico, and as a result he feels that his moral nature is falling into pieces. Duffy's identity and well-ordered room depend on his strength of will, just as Usher's house is a physical expression and extension of Madeline's and Usher's mind. When Usher and Madeline both die, the house, no longer sustained by their spirit, collapses; their controlling or organizing power has gone out of the universe. Usher's house and the tarn, the outermost limits of Usher's universe, are but physical extensions of Usher's own spirit.

Poe's and Joyce's protagonists live in rather unsubstantial mansions and castles. The protagonists themselves are mere abstractions. Their material forms are images of the dark recesses of their souls. Because Poe and Joyce attempt to depict these dark recesses of the soul, they select those mere moments of time, those fancies or "physical impressions" as Poe says in "Marginalia," "when the confines of the waking world blend with those of the world of dreams."[19]

The protagonists of Poe in "The Raven" and Joyce in "Araby" take their departure into the realm of the imagination from books. The protagonists of both writers assume that they are the makers and shapers of their world. The reading of a book makes an image present in their minds. The student sees in the bust of Pallas an emblem of his shaping spirit; likewise, the word "Araby" has a magic power on the boy. Both protagonists evoke then a realm of exotic dreams. The little boy visualizes a statue-like "brown-clad figure cast by [his] imagination." With this image in mind he escapes into the upper part of the house, where "high, cold, empty, gloomy rooms liberated [him] and [he] went from room to room singing."[20] Maria, the laundress in "Clay," has this feeling of freedom when she sings: "I dreamt that I dwelt in marble halls."[21]

For moments of depression, Poe and Joyce choose as inner recesses of their protagonists' souls galleries and dark narrow houses with vaults, caverns, and arches. The protagonists of both writers usually "find themselves" in these recesses. The protagonists of "The Cask of Amontillado" and of the "Narrative of A. Gordon Pym" are lost many times in these caverns and galleries. Similarly, the little boy in "Araby" finds himself in "a big hall girdled at half its height by a gallery. Nearly all the stalls were closed and the greater part of the hall was in darkness."[22] This gallery is an image of frustration. The bareness of the hall means the end of his imaginary voyage.

Galleries and caverns are the terminus of another voyage. The image of galleries returns in the diary entry of "A Portrait of the Artist," revealing Stephen's inward feelings of anxiety and guilt. In his dream, Stephen sees "a long curving gallery. From the floor ascend pillars of dark vapours. It is peopled by the images of fabulous kings, set in stone."[23]

The rooms in Poe's and Joyce's work represent possible facets of the mind. Sometimes their protagonists are caught between their own erroneous reasoning and their imaginings, and they wander through endless numbers of rooms and corridors. In the college of William Wilson there are numberless incomprehensible subdivisions with steps either in ascent or descent in each room, endless windings of corridors, innumerable lateral branches that express all the irrational elements of Wilson's mind.

Similar irrational elements are central in Poe's "The Masque of the Red Death." The irregularly disposed apartments, the "arabesque figures with unsuited limbs and appointments" and the subsequent references to the "most westwardly chamber," "the hall of velvet," "the velvet apartment and the black apartment" suggest that this palace is a coffin. There are also "multitudes of dreams" whose irrational "writhing" steps the wild music seems to echo.[24] This mental incoherence stands as a symbol of the end of the rational order.

In the early Joyce this breakdown of the rational order is indicated in the images of numberless rooms through which the little boy in "Araby" passes. He is irritated by the striking of a clock that contrasts the abandon of the revelry and the rational sobering effect of time.

This rational order is similarly in dissolution in *Stephen Hero*, when Stephen lives in Wilkinson's dilapidated house with fifteen rooms. With the death of Stephen's sister Isabel dissolution invades everything. In his perturbed state, he speaks about sounds, about motions which have no origin save, as Ligeia says, "in the distemper of her fancy, or perhaps in the phantasmagoric influences of the chamber itself."[25] Stephen speaks in the irrational language of Ligeia, saying that

> the chords that floated towards the cobwebs and rubbish and floated vainly to the dust-strewn windows were the meaningless voices of his perturbation and all they could do was flow in meaningless succession through all the chambers of sentience. He breathed an air of tombs.[26]

The coexisting rational and irrational order of the minds of Poe's and Joyce's protagonists is reflected in their close environment. The point of departure is usually a remote room or an isolated house. In this isolation the protagonists live in a world of wild sensations. These sensations are in Poe's imagery preponderantly those of funeral gloom and luxury, whereas those of Joyce, besides the solemnity of funeral gloom, also image the frustrations of the protagonists.

Remote rooms are for Poe's and Joyce's protagonists places of retirement that offer the best opportunities to live their own sensations. In Poe's "The Oval Portrait," the remote turret of a gothic *château* is the frame in which the painter withdraws after the death of his bride. In the high turret of a castellated abbey is Ligeia's bridal chamber in which the resurrected soul of Ligeia

reappears as Lady Rowena. Madeline passes into a remote portion of the apartment after her death in "The Fall of the House
of Usher."

In these remote rooms the protagonists can exist within themselves alone, as the narrator of "The Murders in the Rue Morgue"
emphasizes. For this reason, the protagonist and his friend
Dupin are

> at the expense of renting, and furnishing in a style
> which suited the rather fantastic gloom of our common
> temper, a time-eaten grotesque mansion, long deserted
> through superstitions into which we did not inquire,
> and tottering to its fall in a retired and desolate portion
> of the Faubourg St. Germain.[27]

Joyce, like Poe, uses as setting of his work isolated, remote
rooms, located sometimes on islands, and he shows, in addition
to Poe's use, the frustrations that arise in these remote rooms. As
to the very Poe-like exteriorizations of mental images in Joyce's
work, the remote room reappears in Joyce's "The Sisters" several
times: a priest dies in a very remote room and Stephen imagines
he sees the heavy grey face of the paralytic in his remote dark
room. This image of Stephen's mind is exteriorized when he
believes he sees the priest sitting in a little dark remote room
behind the shop called "Drapery."

The setting of "Araby" suggests frustration. The action starts
in North Richmond Street, a blind street, in an uninhabited
house, at the blind end, detached from its neighbors. There a
priest has died in a back drawing room. Sitting in a remote, bare
railway carriage, Stephen is frustrated when the train moves out
of the station after an intolerable delay and finally draws up to
an "improvised wooden platform" at "ten to ten." This flatness
of time and space suggests the boy's helplessness and the notion
that he has arrived in a region out of time and out of space. The
dream ends in the bareness of a darkened, suburban bazaar.

The setting of "The Dead" in "the dark, gaunt house on Usher's
Island, the upper part of which they had rented from Mr. Ful-
ham, the corn factor on the ground floor,"[28] with its dark stairs,

crevices and folds, with an old piano in the backroom, and with remote corners recalls the architecture and isolation of Poe's House of Usher.

The remoteness from familiar objects and the romantic world outside of Eveline's sickroom reveals the contrast of concrete and abstract reality. For a long time she has been separated from her familiar objects. She distinguishes sharply the reality of her mind from the world outside by depicting the clacking foot-steps on "concrete pavements" and the brown houses of reality in contrast to the "crunching" footsteps on the "cinder path," and "the bright brick houses with shining roofs."[29] Eveline, like Poe's Berenice or Eleanora, lives in a transcendental world of her mental life. She is divided from the real, romantic world like little Chandler in Joyce's "A Little Cloud"; the Poe-like image of the absence of an "organic community" frustrates little Chandler in the "mansions in which the old nobility of Dublin had roystered."[30]

These remote houses are physical extensions of the protago-nists' own spirits. These mansions and houses with shining roofs, these remote rooms and cinder paths are very unsubstantial, are abstractions of reality. Poe and Joyce concretize their ideas in these mental images of mansions and rooms. When Usher's sister Madeline dies, his room bears witness of his profuse, comfort-less, antique, and tottered mind. In *Stephen Hero* Stephen feels the same effect of antiquity, decay, neglect and dissolution after the death of his sister Isabel. He retires to Mr. Wilkinson's lofty, dusty drawing room panelled with oak. Sitting at the piano "while the sunless dusk enwrapped him," he "could feel about him and above him the hopeless house and the decay of leaves and in his soul the one bright insistent star of joy trembling at her wane."[31]

In these remote rooms feelings of the loss of identity arise, and thoughts of death preoccupy the minds of the protagonists. In the "Hades" episode in *Ulysses*, Dublin itself is presented as the kingdom of the dead. "The Irishman's house is a coffin."[32] Thoughts of death are in everybody's mind. This world of the dead parallels Poe's concept of a world outside of concrete reality, a world out of space and time.

Poe's and Joyce's images of a dead world are artistic media for the concretization of their ideas. These ideas become visualizations, as we find them expressed by Stephen in the "Scylla" episode and by Poe in "Some Words with a Mummy."[33] Stephen thinks: "Coffined thoughts around me, in mummycases, embalmed in spice of words. Thoth, god of libraries, a birdgod, moony-crowned. And I heard the voice of the Egyptian high priest. *In painted chambers loaded with tilebooks.*"[34] This last observation, "*In painted chambers loaded with tilebooks*" suggests that coffined thoughts are expressed as visualizations in chambers. These thoughts, confined to "mummycases," recall Poe's coffin-shaped case of the Egyptian mummy, in which funeral scenes, interspersed with certain hieroglyphic characters, are a social commentary, directed haphazardly at man's vaunted theory of inevitable progress. Hence the thoughts, confined for Poe and Joyce in "mummycases," have allegorical meaning. This meaning, confined in Poe's and Joyce's work to the narrow boundaries of pictures, establishes further affinities between the two writers.

Imagery of Lighting

Poe and Joyce set out lighting designs that are carefully planned and executed. They show in the way they arrange rooms and define shape and proportions of windows that they use ingenious methods of lighting. The effects are produced by well-calculated quantities and qualities of lights that are arranged and blended into the scene or story line. Light and shadow are for them similar constituents that function to create color atmosphere as in the impressionist paintings, or to focus the attention of the eyes upon one scene, as for example in Rembrandt's chiaroscuro. In these instances light and shadow are modifications of color.

Besides these modifications of color, Poe and Joyce use the effects of light and shadow for purposes of plot, rare decoration, for an expression of dementia, or for funeral feasts. Observing these effects, Poe and Joyce regard shadows as expressing foreboding and insecurity and lights as expressing transparent symbols of security. The effects of light and shadow appear in their work in images of daytime, of nighttime, and of chiaroscuro.

Two aspects of the images of daytime and nighttime are reflected in Poe's and Joyce's imagery of lighting in the contrast of emotion and reason: the one aspect shows the obscure minds of their protagonists in the dark torment of nightmare, the other represents them lucid and inquiring, eager to explain real and concrete matter of a thoroughly prosaic kind. The distinction between emotion and reason is reflected in the form of nighttime images in the objects of imaginative perception and in the form of daytime images in the actual objects of the external world.

Chiaroscuro serves Poe and Joyce first of all to suggest ghastly presences that reveal the states of anxiety, suffocation, and helplessness of the protagonists.

All these effects of light suggest similarities between Poe's and Joyce's imagery. These similarities consist

    (a.) in the technique of spotlighting;
    (b.) in the image associations of lights, colors, and space;
    (c.) in images of radiance;
    (d.) in the associated images of bright lights and emotions;
    (e.) in the contrasts of images of light and darkness;
    (f.) in the images of dread;
    (g.) in the images of livid lights and destruction;
    (h.) in the images of whiteness, a light without prismatic reflection, and paralysis.

These groups of images will be the center of the following discussion.

Poe and Joyce light up specific spots of interest, be they outdoors or indoors. They use lights which are flaming, glaring, writhing, sputtering, frightening, brooding, or just flickering and burning pallidly and motionlessly. These lights are used as spotlights.

Poe views landscapes by "a gate of vista," as he explains it in "The Domain of Arnheim." He looks at reality from one specific point under the changing lights of day. Indoor spotlighting focuses on very small areas in spite of the vastness of chambers or halls in which the actions take place. Poe restricts the effusion of light to a narrow section. A photograph, a picture, a table, or a fireplace is picked up by the flicker of a candle, the red glow of a torch or flambeau or by the dim wavering of a lamp. In "Shadow—A Parable" he lets the candle shine just brightly enough upon the brass door. In "Ms. Found in a Bottle" the candle is a phenomenal flickerless omen. In "The Oval Portrait" it etches the light and shadow print.

Joyce also adopts this method of spotlighting and uses these artificial light effects in an ever-improving technique. He does not use any spotlights in *Stephen Hero*, but shows all things in daylight. In his later work, Joyce replaces daylight by spotlight. In "Ivy Day in the Committee Room" he introduces candles to light the bareness of the room of the particular point of the story:

> A denuded room came into view and the fire lost all its cheerful colour. The walls of the room were bare except for a copy of an election address. In the middle of the room was a small table on which papers were heaped.[35]

Little Chandler in "A Little Cloud" by Joyce pays attention to a picture, because light falls on it, when it is sitting in the "room off the hall."[36]

In "A Portrait of the Artist" we are looking at a room through a keyhole instead of through an open door. As in Poe's tales, the vague shapes in the dark corners add portentousness to what our framed and limited vision can perceive.

Hard, bright, artificial light floods the Dublin of *Ulysses*. We see the city as a whole. Here life and oriental splendor, death and decay are never isolated from the effects of light. Thus in the "Calypso" episode we see that the sunburst is to Bloom a symbol of oriental splendor, while grey twilight, a cloud over the sun, is an image of the shadow of death. Throughout the episode there is a rhythmic interplay of shadow and sunlight that recalls vividly Poe's Valley of Unrest in "Eleanora."

In the successive episodes of *Finnegans Wake* the effects of light on the material surroundings become less and less clear and parallel the sleep of the protagonist by "sinking deeper and deeper into the swamp of the night-mind, joining the mud-encrusted memories of earlier months and years, and allying themselves with obscurer psychic forces."[37] Thus in Earwicker's night-world the gloomy lights parallel the lubricious sermon of Sham the Post, harbinger of the New Day:

> Shoot up on that, bright Bennu bird! *Va faotre!* Eftsoon so too will our own sphoenix spark spirt his spyre and sunward stride the rampante flambe. Ay, already the sombrer opacities of the gloom are spanished! brave footsore Haun! Work your progress! Hold to! Now! Win out, ye divil ye! The silent cock shall crow at last. The west shall shake the east awake. Walk while ye have the night for morn, lightbreakfastbringer, morroweth whereon every past shall full fost asleep. Amain.[38]

Poe and Joyce see, through the use of spotlights, objects in space like a picture, illuminated by one source of light. They illuminate only those objects by which their protagonists are effected. They reduce thereby all things to their degree of visibility in space.

Poe in "Eleanora" perceives the outside world in terms of what the eye can see, of pure visibility, under spotlights, and as a reflection of the psyche of the protagonists: "the light . . . peered at noon-day into the centre of the valley."[39] In "The Domain of Arnheim" Poe depicts the essences of a circular valley in terms of its fluctuating colors, as seen in space:

> This basin was of great depth, but so transparent was the water that the bottom, which seemed to consist of a thick mass of small round alabaster pebbles, was distinctly visible by glimpses—that is to say, whenever the eye could permit itself *not* to see, far down in the inverted heaven, the duplicate blooming of the hills . . .

but as the eye traced upward the myriad-tinted slope, from its sharp junction with the water to its vague termination amid the folds of overhanging cloud, it became, indeed, difficult not to fancy a panoramic cataract of rubies, sapphires, opals, and golden onyxes, rolling silently out of the sky.[40]

This type of space perception that Poe describes with shades of colors, Joyce observes similarly. Joyce, like Poe and the modern impressionist painters, does not see the body's plastic nature, but shows only concepts and associations that are directly given to sight by the effects of light and dark shades. The light that Joyce throws in "Grace" on an assembly in the church makes visible their "black clothes and white collars, relieved here and there by tweeds, on dark mottled pillars of green marble and on lugubrious canvases."[41] Joyce also withholds from the evocations of figures all the ideas that cannot be reduced to sheer sight. In "The Dead" he raises this question:

> He asked himself what is a woman standing on the stairs in the shadow, listening to distant music, a symbol of. If he were a painter, he would paint her in that attitude. Her blue felt hat would show off the bronze of her hair against the darkness and the dark panels of her skirt would show off the light ones. *Distant music* he would call the picture if he were a painter.[42]

Our mind here is deprived of all concepts and associations not given directly to sight.

Joyce sees shadows in full color. He uses these color effects of shadows in *Ulysses*, in the interior monologue, as Budgen points out:

> The whole is built up out of nuances instead of being constructed in broad masses, things are seen as immersed in a luminous fluid; color supplies the modelling, and the total effect is arrived at through a countless number of small touches. Like impressionist art . . . it is an effort to approach reality.[43]

As the images of Poe's and Joyce's work show, both writers perceive the outside world in terms of pure visibility. The world, seen in dark and bright shades, is for Stephen no longer objectively determined; he perceives mental associations that belong to his subconscious world as he expresses it in *Ulysses*:

> Ineluctable modality of the visible: at least that if no more, thought through my eyes. Signatures of all things I am here to read, seaspawn and seawrack, the nearing tide, that rusty boot. Snotgreen, bluesilver, rust: coloured signs. Limits of the diaphane. But he adds: in bodies.[44]

Diaphane is light when actualized and darkness when potential. It is the medium that makes color visible while color makes the diaphane itself visible.

Poe's and Joyce's images create the impression of a continual meditation on the nature of space and the distribution of light. Objects appear to have radiance, and spread their luminous effects on the surrounding world. This radiance is gloomy as Usher observes:

> And thus, as a closer intimacy admitted me more unreservedly into the recesses of this spirit, the more bitterly did I perceive the futility of all attempt at cheering a mind from which darkness, as if an inherent positive quality, poured forth upon all objects of the moral and physical universe in one unceasing radiation of gloom.[45]

This kind of radiation also streamed forth from the picture that

> presented the interior of an immensely long and rectangular vault or tunnel, with low walls, smooth, white, and without interruption or device. Certain accessory points of the design served well to convey the idea that this excavation lay at an exceeding depth below the surface of the earth. No outlet was observed in any portion of its vast extent, and no torch or other artificial source of light was discernible; yet a flood of intense rays rolled throughout, and bathed the whole in a ghastly and inappropriate splendor.[46]

This painting forecasts the subterranean vault in which the body of Usher's sister will be placed.

A similar type of radiance is a device that Joyce uses throughout his work. In *Ulysses* he uses radiance as a device to forecast a later scene in much the same way as Poe did.

> The summer evening had begun to fold the world in its mysterious embrace. Far away in the west the sun was setting and the last glow of all too fleeting day lingered lovingly on sea and strand, on the proud promontory of dear old Howth guarding as ever the waters of the bay, on the weedgrown rocks along Sandymount shore and, last but not least, on the quiet church whence there streamed forth at times upon the stillness the voice of prayer to her who is in her pure radiance a beacon ever to the stormtossed heart of man, Mary, star of the sea.[47]

In this passage the Head of Howth guards the bay in the mode of God become rock; the Protean strand of early morning has set and hardened, like the souls of Dubliners, into "weedgrown rocks." The Virgin Mary is seen as the "beacon ever to the stormtossed heart of man," an image that receives later its material incorporation in "The Oxen of the Sun" episode.

These images of Poe and Joyce show that the objects of a purely visual contemplation are luminous. The form of these objects is described as *rayonnement* and seems to affect the eyes, most of all as pure visibility.

These images of light express the clarity of the minds of the protagonists. Their powers of reasoning are stimulated in the lights of crowded cities where they hope to find excitement, knowledge, and happiness. Similarly attracted by lights is the protagonist in "The Man of the Crowd," by Poe. When twilight comes, the man constantly plunges into the midst of crowds filled with trembling lights and shadows; he flees from the quiet and peaceful places and eargerly goes in search of those that swarm with human activity. As the circle of life and light grows smaller, he seeks the center with a feeling of anxiety.

Crowded cities at night attract Poe's protagonists, Dupin and

Virag, who wish to find there some enlightenment. This search
for enlightenment is the reason for Stephen's attempt to find
amidst the cities' crowds knowledge and sensations.

In Joyce's "Araby" Stephen wanders through flaring streets,
since "the noises converged in a single sensation of life for me
[Stephen]."[48] Even a look at a strange-looking city and at ships
make Stephen happy.[49] Stephen does not mind all the gloomy
streets in order to reach the lighted, crowded center of excitement.

> It would be a gloomy secret night. After early nightfall
> the yellow lamps would light up, here and there, the
> squalid quarter of the brothels. He would follow a de-
> vious course up and down the streets, circling always
> nearer and nearer in a tremor of fear and joy, until his
> feet led him suddenly round a dark corner.[50]

As in "The Man of the Crowd" the center of light and life awake
feelings of anxiety in Stephen.

Light, image of joy and happiness, forms the middle section
of "The Dead." The first section shows the arrival of the people
from out of the snow-filled landscape of Dublin, and the last
section describes their return to the world of snow. The light,
music, and cheer of the middle section contrast sharply with the
bleak coldness of the two parts which set the frame for it. The
Christmas festivity that is an oasis of warmth and life shut off
from the surrounding world outside recalls the festivities of "The
Masque of the Red Death" by Poe in the isolation of a castellated abbey.

Thus Poe and Joyce show in these images how lighted,
crowded sites attract the protagonists in their search for knowledge, reason, and sensations.

Poe contrasts darkness and light in "Ms. Found in a Bottle,"
where the light imagery is placed against the pitch black whirlpool. "The Assignation" has likewise an extreme contrast, that
between absolute darkness and murky water and flaring torches.
"Silence—A Fable" places its concentration on darkness that is
unrelieved except by the lurid, diabolical red of sun and moon, a

scene in which any bright images would be out of keeping. The dark backgrounds of all these images account also for the heavy predominance of "dark" generic terms, such as shadow, darkness, and gloom.

This contrast of light and darkness relates Poe's imagery to that of Joyce, who also achieved similar effects in presenting gloomy, dark images of reality in contrast to the bright images, light and fire, of his visions. In "The Sisters" there is a lighted square of an upstairs window which is studied in anticipation of its eclipse by the darkened blind of the dead room. In "Counterparts" the dark image of shadow is repeated and contrasted to the light of a lamp. O'Halloran, very discontented, returns home along the shadow of the walls. When he sees his son, the contrast of light and darkness is stressed in the remark: "Light the lamp. What do you mean by having the place in darkness?"[51] Light and darkness contrast the happy illusions of a world of dreams with the bareness of reality in "Araby." A distant lamp attracts the little boy in "Araby" to leave his home, and his trip ends in a bazaar that turns out to be just as cold, as dark, and as man-made as the gloomy house of the dead priest in the little boy's own street. In "Clay" the theme is reiterated, when Maria, a laundress, living in a dark surrounding sings "I dreamt that I dwelt in marble halls."[52] In "A Portrait of the Artist" the dark colors of the location of Blackrock are contrasted with the small whitewashed house of Stephen's friend Mercedes.

Images of nighttime and chiaroscuro create in Poe's and Joyce's work an atmosphere of gloomy remorse and twisted desires. The images of darkness and chiaroscuro are combined with images of dread and fear. Both writers depict the innermost recesses of their protagonists in the dark nights of fear. This fear arises from dark presences that are a dread to the helpless protagonists. This feeling of dread inheres in the dark and gloomy atmosphere that Poe and Joyce depict in similar images.

Some protagonists live in the gloomy atmosphere of twilight. The feelings of fear in darkness are most expressive when they appear in connection with the many allusions to cold and dampness, as they do in the caverns and galleries through which Pym,

Montresor, and Wilson in Poe's tales and Stephen in Joyce's work are wandering.

Beside these images of dread that arise in chiaroscuro, images of dissolution and sickness arise in a chiaroscuro of grey and dull shades. This dissolution is often reflected in the eyes of the protagonists. Usher's eyes are dull and are paralleled by the vacant eye-like windows of the house. These eyes suggest dissolution, as Baudelaire's translation of this passage shows. He translates these eye-like windows by "les fenêtres semblables à des yeux distraits."[53] The meaning of these dull eyes is communicated in terms of distraction, a stage of dissolution. Madeline Usher's eyes and those of Berenice, when they fall sick, are dull and lack lustre. Similarly, when Valdemar attempts to ward off death's utter destruction, his eyes are lustreless.

These dull shades that Poe associates with the lustre of eyes, Joyce connects with the atmosphere in which Stephen lives. By the dull atmosphere Joyce communicates the idea of sickness. In "A Portrait of the Artist" the images of swift December dusk, the dull day, the dull square of the window of the schoolroom forecast the idea of sickness.[54] This sickness is reflected in the universe when "the stars began to crumble and a cloud of fine stardust fell through space. The dull light fell more faintly . . . and the cold darkness filled chaos."[55]

Dullness also expresses uncertainty and fear. This uncertainty and fear are reflected in Usher's dull eyes before his dissolution. Similarly, Stephen's heart in the dull atmosphere, in the dull light of the college retreat, "began slowly to fold and fade with fear like a withering flower."[56] "In the silence their dark fire kindled the dusk into the tawny glow. Stephen's heart had withered up like a flower of the desert that feels the simoom coming from afar."[57] Fear and anxiety oppress Stephen more and more, and soon, like Poe's narrator in "Loss of Breath," he is able to perceive only threatening dusk:

> His [Stephen's] soul was flattening and congealing into
> a gross grease, plunging ever deeper in its dull fear into
> a sombre threatening dusk, while the body that was his

stood, listless and dishonored, gazing out of darkened eyes, helpless, perturbed and human for a bovine to stare upon.[58] .

Livid lights associated with images of shrill sounds announce the destruction of the universe in Poe's and Joyce's work.

Poe uses livid lights deliberately in "Silence,"[59] when the heaven became livid with the violence of a tempest. In "Bon-Bon" the image of snow is combined with the destruction of the earth: "It snowed fiercely, and the house tottered to its centre with the floods of wind . . . rushing through the crannies of the wall. . . ."[60]

Stephen in *Ulysses* announces the end of the world in livid flames: "He lifts his ashplant high with both hands and smashes the chandelier. Time's livid final flame leaps and, in the following darkness, ruin of all space, shattered glass and toppling masonry."[61] Stephen is thus the destroyer of light, because he smashes the lamp.

The destruction of Dublin is depicted by Joyce in the "Circe" episode. The livid flames destroy Nighttown, the city of darkness, the darkness of which has affected the whole life of Dublin. There is a cry of "Police" and distant voices call: "Dublin's burning! Dublin's burning! On fire, On Fire!"[62]

These images illustrate the fact that Poe and Joyce associate livid lights with the destruction of the world.

The images of lights and whiteness unify organic and inorganic matter in a harmonious whole. The concept of whiteness is related to a state of absence. This state of absence expresses an unbearable terror. As the complete absence of sound in "Silence —A Fable" expresses such terror, so does the complete absence of color. The ramparts of white ice at the end of "Ms. Found in a Bottle" are terrifying, and the protagonists are incapable of re-action. There is a belt of white surf beating against the rocky shore and the white foam encircling the black whirlpool in "A Descent into the Maelstrom" which draws the helpless protagonists into its center. This paralysis that the white circles call forth in the protagonists is widened in the "Narrative of A. Gordon

Pym." In this narrative the external world becomes more and more a sharp distinction between white (of the sea, the polar bear, the sky) and black (the natives, the terrain). At the end of the journey Pym is sailing toward the whiteness of the purest unknown. Pym and Peter perceive the graying vapor in the air, the milkiness of the water, the rain of fine white powder resembling ashes, the flight of many gigantic and pallidly white birds. Pym and Peter are powerless to take action when they rush toward the endless cataract. This cataract is of purest whiteness: it is a color without any body and light without any prismatic reflection. Thus all matter has yielded in the final image of the "Narrative of A. Gordon Pym" to the brightness of white space. The narrative comes to a sudden halt, after recording a vision of a white face: ". . . there arose in our pathway a shrouded human figure . . . the hue of the skin of the figure was of the perfect whiteness of the snow."[63]

This image of whiteness relates Pym's vision closely to the final image of snow in "Dubliners," "The Dead." The image of whiteness, be it the milky sea in the "Narrative of A. Gordon Pym" or snow in "The Dead," overwhelms everything in sameness and death. The identity of the protagonists fades out thus into the white and impalpable world. This whiteness, as already mentioned, is light without any prismatic reflection and color without body.

In "A Portrait of the Artist" by Joyce the light of the day is as weak as Stephen's body.

> The evening air was pale and chilly and after every charge and thud of the footballers the greasy leather orb flew like a heavy bird through the grey light. He kept on the fringe of his line, out of sight of his prefect, out of the reach of the rude feet, feigning to run now and then. He felt his body small and weak amid the throng of players and his eyes were weak and watery.[64]

Throughout the first two chapters of the book, Joyce heavily accents his use of the color white, and each time white is associated either with a feeling of revulsion or with blind obedience to some code.

In Poe's and Joyce's imagery whiteness is associated with a state of paralysis or imperfection. One could compare this image of whiteness with the physical, mental, and spiritual capacities of the protagonists. Just as white is color without body and as light is without prismatic reflection, thus matter is without body; so Poe's and Joyce's protagonists in their early stages in the story are persons without will to react, without any physical capacities and without identity. They fade out into the whiteness of snow or the milky sea, into states of sameness and nothingness.

The objects and perceptions of the external world serve Poe and Joyce for a progressive deepening spiritualization. With the romantics and surrealists they try to get beneath the surface, starting from stable and objective elements which they apprehend in their pure states. In the way they go beyond reality, they extend the range of their vision.

CHAPTER FOUR

The Images of Paralysis, Perverseness, and Wild Sensations

The Images of Paralysis

From the moral point of view, paralysis is a condition of having partially or totally lost the faculties of sensation and voluntary motion. Paralysis is an atrophy of the powers of decision. Therefore paralysis is basically a default of the will.

The will, according to an aphorism of Glanvill, quoted by Poe in "Ligeia," determines whether man is able to control himself and master the exterior world: "man doth not yield himself to the angels, nor unto death utterly, save only through the weakness of his feeble will."[1] Poe and Joyce illustrate in similar images man's struggle to triumph over mere mortality or paralysis by the strength of the will.

When the will is passive, the individual falls a victim of the surrounding world, which means decay, death and paralysis. Mental and physical death descends upon the protagonists, because they do not act; this inertia is reflected in the surrounding world in images of decay and lifelessness.

Basically, there are two forms of paralysis that are predominant in Poe's and Joyce's work:

1. Paralysis of the protagonist's will to change the conditions of the surrounding world in which he lives, as is exemplified by Usher and the protagonists of "Dubliners."

2. Paralysis of the ability to keep up the stableness of the individual's tripartite being of body, mind, and spirit that leads to the final decay of the individual, as is exemplified by Poe's William Wilson and Joyce's Stephen in *Stephen Hero*.

"Usher," as Davidson points out, "saw around him the infinite interrelations of the self and the world outside; he lived in such terror that his private mind-being might be destroyed that he created the outer protective shell or the House."[2] Usher attempts to counteract the fear of hereditary madness and dissolution by seeking refuge in opium; the drug paralyzes his capacity of mental decision even more, so that eventually the temporary therapeutic escapes of painting and music fail him. Finally he is so paralyzed with fear and drugs that he cannot move even one step out of Madeline's way.

Horror also overpowers William Wilson, who becomes a complete victim of the other self:

> Thus far I had succumbed to this imperious domination. The sentiment of deep awe with which I habitually regarded the elevated character, the majestic wisdom, the apparent omnipresence and omnipotence of Wilson, added to a feeling of even terror . . . had operated, hitherto, to impress me with an idea of my own utter weakness and helplessness, and to suggest an implicit, although bitterly reluctant submission to his arbitrary will.[2]

Wilson and Usher do not have, as these examples illustrate, enough power of will to control their surrounding world.

Poe's protagonists live in a world of horror. In this world men are moral mutes or paralytics, unable to change the conditions in which they live. In the "Narrative of A. Gordon Pym" there are situations in which human will is powerless to effect any variations of its own existence. The action widens more and more from the focus of the sailing port of Nantucket and Pym's self-controlled life to the final loss of individuality by the total paralysis of the senses and, concurrently, by the steady dissolution of the world of physical reality:

> A storm was evidently behind us [Pym and Augustus]; we had neither compass nor provisions; and it was clear that, if we held our present course, we should be out of sight of land before daybreak. These thoughts, with a

crowd of others, equally fearful, flashed through my mind with bewildering rapidity, and for some moments paralyzed me beyond the possibility of making any exertion. . . . I tumbled headlong and insensible upon the body of my fallen companion.[3]

Pym and Augustus are unable to give signals to the brig that passes by and would rescue them from their situation. Terror-stricken by the vision of a smiling, eyeless face, all their faculties of the mind are prostrated and they can "neither think nor act."[4]

Another form of paralysis appears in "Ligeia," when the protagonist is at "the verge of remembrance,"[5] without being able, in the end, to remember. There is for the protagonist no possibility of fathoming the mystery which "Ligeia" symbolizes, though in the height of passionate adoration he feels himself to be "upon the very verge," which experience he likens to that of almost but not quite recalling something from the depths of his unconscious.

The inability of the will to dictate to the unconscious and its inability to dictate to love reveals something more than the hero's vague awareness of a psychic flaw which thwarts his desire. This inability reveals the source of the obsession of the protagonist in the struggle to achieve by power of mind what he cannot achieve through love. The passage from Glanvill is the key, the psychic formula, which he hopes may open to him the very mystery of being, his own as well as Ligeia's.

Another type of paralysis is depicted in connection with the reanimation of Ligeia. The horror felt by the protagonist leads to the suspension of the normal, rational faculties of thinking and choice. The protagonist feels the need that

some immediate exertion be made; yet the turret was altogether apart from the portion of the abbey tenanted by the servants—there were none within call—I had no means of summoning them to my aid without leaving the room for many minutes—and this I could not venture to do.[6]

The protagonist is in a helpless situation and soon complete paralysis overpowers him as it did Usher:

> I [the protagonist of "Ligeia"] trembled not—I stirred not—for a crowd of unutterable fancies connected with the air, the stature, the demeanor, of the figure, rushing hurriedly through my brain, had paralyzed—had chilled me into stone. I stirred not—but I gazed upon the apparition.[7]

A similar version of paralysis, a result of a vision of horror, is to be found in "The Conversation of Eiros and Charmion" and in "The Colloquy of Monos and Una." The characters are victims of an apocalypse which has had no perceptible reason for being, and their intellect is hypertrophied. Thereby their emotions and moral senses are weakened. The two tales are rationalizations of horror, as Davidson points out:

> the principle of horror itself seems to imply that the horrific is that which suddenly interrupts or shatters the rational order of the universe; however completely that order is restored, the human mind forced to endure that "apocalypse" or shock and will be forever dislocated or maddened.[8]

Joyce depicts a similar apocalyptic earthquake at the end of *Ulysses*, when the decay of society and religion embraces the earth itself.[9] This decay finds its strongest expression in the final image of dissolution and madness.

Paralysis is one of the key images of Poe's and Joyce's work. Joyce wrote in a letter to Grant Richards:

> My intention was to write a chapter of the moral history of my country and I chose Dublin for the scene because that city seemed to be the centre of paralysis. I have tried to present it to the indifferent public under four of its aspects: childhood, adolescence, maturity and public life.[10]

Paralysis is the key image not only to "Dubliners" but also to *Stephen Hero* and "A Portrait of the Artist as a Young Man." In *Stephen Hero* Joyce stresses the paralysis produced by Catholicism in Ireland: "an island (whereof)) the inhabitants of which entrust their wills and minds to others that they may ensure for themselves a life of spiritual paralysis. . . ."[11]

Because of this spiritual paralysis, Joyce's work deals essentially with evil, perverseness, atrophy of powers, with physical ugliness and decay. These are at the same time the major themes of Poe's work.

With these artistic devices Poe and Joyce illustrate the three main components of a human personality: the mental, physical and spiritual faculties. If one of these faculties is paralyzed, then the individual is prone to death. Such cases Poe represents in the above-mentioned forms of paralysis.

In close affinity to these forms of paralysis Joyce shows how the intellect overwhelms emotions and how the will is unable to dictate love in "A Painful Case." The main character, Duffy, is an intellectual who has allowed his study to separate him from the world of other human beings. Significantly, his face has the impersonal brown tint of Dublin streets. He lives "at a little distance from his body"[12] because he has neatly catalogued life and has filled all of experience into the proper categories in his mind. His world is as neat, as ordered and impersonal as his room. This room is the platonic idea of a room; it is always kept spotlessly white and in order, because he "abhorred anything which betokened physical and mental disorder."[13] Therefore, after a short romance with Mrs. Sinico, Mr. Duffy concludes that we cannot give ourselves. He indulges in a life of isolation, being emotionally as dead to the world as are Poe's women, such as Ligeia, Morella or Berenice.

On the other hand, Poe and Joyce depict characters who are unable to change their own situation. Thus in "Dubliners," the protagonists, like Usher, are usually defeated by the combined forces of their environment. Eveline Hill, for example, is offered an escape from a life like her mother's composed of "commonplace sacrifices closing in final craziness." Thoughts of her mother put "powerful hands on her, goading her towards escape" with her friend, a sailor. She plans to elope with him to Buenos Aires. "He would give her life, perhaps love, too. But she wanted to live."[14] At the crucial moment however, her resolution drains away, and her plan fails to materialize. At the quay, when her sailor beckons her towards the ship, she draws back, suddenly terrified at the thought of freedom. The net is too strong for her to break through, and she shrinks back into the captivity of family and past. When she stands on the pier, "she set her white face to him, passive like a helpless animal." The main reason why Eveline fails is that she does not will to act. This lack of will to act establishes an affinity to the frustrations that Poe's protagonists must undergo.

This lack of determination to take action is also encountered in "After the Race," in the image of clumps of people who are the passive observers of the race. Here the effect of inertia is heightened by the contrasting image of speed:

> And through this channel of poverty and inaction the continent sped its wealth and industry. Now and again the clumps of people raised the cheer of the gratefully oppressed.[15]

At the end the spectators are completely paralyzed by terror: The spectators are set into a dark stupor by the terrible game.[16] In this short-story motion is only apparent. The protagonists, Jimmy and his family, are as paralyzed as Eveline. The family is caught in a social paralysis and will never realize it.

Unable to change his situation at home, Little Chandler of Joyce's "A Little Cloud" is convinced that he could do better if he had a chance. He has no will to assume authority. In "The Sisters" Joyce ascribes this lack of strength of will to the spiritual guardians of the country. The Roman Catholic priest does not have strength of will since his breaking of the chalice. On his deathbed, his large hands are only "loosely retaining the chalice."[17] This image closes "The Sisters:" "I knew," says the boy narrator, "that the old priest was lying still in his coffin as we have seen him, solemn and truculent in death, an idle chalice on his breast."[18] The chalice would not have been broken had it not been kept loosely in the large idle hands of the priest. The priest is the representative of the church. Hence not only the priest but also the church is meant to be morally sick. This sickness is represented in the weak will of the priest.

Besides this example of the spiritual paralysis of the country, Joyce opens also some aspects of the political paralysis that hovers over Ireland. In "Ivy Day in the Committee Room" the visitors in the committee room are all prey to the same lethargy; the men are politically impotent. All action is paralyzed.

All these cases, as we have seen, are a result of the weakness of the volitional powers. Family life, priesthood, politics, the individual, the crowd, they all are morally sick, since they lack the will to change their own condition. They are paralytics in regard to mental, emotional, or physical capacities. Although Joyce broadens the images by which Poe presented his paralytics, his images basically reflect what Poe wished to express: that the triumph of the will of the protagonist over paralysis determines the life or death of any social relation.

This death, as Robert Stanley Ryf points out,

> represents figurative as well as literal unaliveness. Gabriel, although physically alive, is emotionally dead. Gretta, once emotionally alive in her relationship with Michael Furey, is now emotionally dead, although physically alive. And Michael, once emotionally alive, is now physically dead. Thus Joyce, relating the emotional life to the physical, suggests a vital correspondence between the two. Emotional death becomes living death.[19]

Gabriel contrasts the will to die with the passive, frustrating dying away without emotions. When he thinks of his family in "The Dead" he shows that

> one by one, they were all becoming shades. Better pass boldly into that other world, in the full glory of some passion, than fade and wither dismally with age.[20]

Gabriel appreciates the fact that Michael Furey has died in the glory of his passion for Gretta. Such an end is no longer possible for Gabriel, since he is now emotionally sterile. It is a lack of will that makes him emotionally passive and paralyzes him to such an extent that he can only wither dismally into death.

As Gabriel is standing before the window he sees that snow is falling through the universe; he feels his own identity fading out into a grey and impalpable world, "dissolving and dwindling."[21] The doom of paralysis is the fate of all men. In the final image Joyce has expanded the entire book into a moral history of mankind of which "Dubliners" is only one specific manifestation.

In "Dubliners" Joyce shows like Poe that the protagonists are dead if they lack enough strength of will to improve their mental, physical and psychological shortcomings.

Poe's and Joyce's characters in these situations are "dead." In *The Forlorn Demon* Tate very significantly points out that Poe's characters are

> in the words of William Wilson's double, "dead to the world," they are machines of sensations and will, with correspondences in the physical universe to particles and energy. Poe's engrossing obsession in *Eureka* with the cosmic destiny of man issued in a quasi-cosmology, a more suitable extension of his vision than any mythology, home-made or traditional, could have offered him.[22]

From this point of view we may also consider the final vision of Gabriel as an image not of individual death, but of the death of the universe.

Poe and Joyce associate paralysis with death: the paralysis of the individual with the death of the world. Paralysis hovers over Poe's and Joyce's characters and their environment. Furniture, houses, rooms, nature and human beings are all dead. This deadness of the world Joyce states on the first page to "The Sisters"; and he introduces three expressions for it:

1. Simony, referring to the death of the church and imaging the spiritual death of mankind;
2. Gnomon, expressing the only partially perfect condition of

organic or inorganic matter, imaging the physical death of the organic and inorganic world;

3. Paralysis, the psychological and intellectual death of humanity.

All these three expressions taken together may be reduced to one common denominator: the atrophy of one of the intellectual, physical, or spiritual faculties. Poe and Joyce depict the failures of these classical faculties: feeling, will, and intellect. The failures of these natural faculties lead to frustrations. These frustrations are the main themes of Poe's and Joyce's work. As to "Dubliners," each of the characters in this book is a failure because he does not will to act or because he does not act. In their failure to take counteraction, the protagonists are always defeated by the combined forces of their environment.

The aphorism of Glanvill that Poe quotes in an epigraph to "Ligeia" is characteristically, as mentioned previously, a leading theme in Poe's and Joyce's work: "Man doth not yield himself to the angels, nor unto death utterly, save only through the weakness of his feeble will."[23] Poe's and Joyce's protagonists are captives, prisoners of this life. Their will power is too inefficient to change religious, political, and social conditions. This atrophy of the volitional powers links Joyce closely to Poe, for both illustrate in their images that individuals are in their primary states unable to will a change of their conditions.

Poe and Joyce represent these captives in two similar images by associating the images of paralysis and the coffin. The image of the coffined priest, sitting in "his confession-box, wide-awake and laughing-like softly to himself"[24] recalls the image of one of the paralyzed persons in "King Pest" by Poe. Poe, like Joyce, expresses in this image of physical arrest the idea of moral paralysis. These two images of coffined persons are images of living death. Both characters are "dead to the World,"[25] hence dead to their environment.

The environment has either paralyzing or stimulating influences on the sensibility of the protagonists in Poe's and Joyce's work as the following images, taken as obvious examples, show.

Wilson grows up with weak-minded parents who have constitutional infirmities. Hence Wilson is left to the guidance of his own will: "I [Wilson] was left to the guidance of my own will, and became, in all but name, the master of my own actions."[26] When Wilson enters school his will to take action is paralyzed daily. Not only do the prison-like ramparts around the domain have mortifying effects on Wilson, but also the meeting with his double. Finally, by an impulse of perverseness he has lost all control over his will and is forced to kill his double.

Although Joyce does not represent any image of a similar act of perverseness in the mortifying frame of the atmosphere of the school, he illustrates how the college atmosphere breaks the will of Stephen to believe in Catholicism.

> The deadly chill of the atmosphere of the college paralysed Stephen's heart. In a stupor of powerlessness he reviewed the plague of Catholicism. He seemed to see the vermin begotten in the catacombs in an age of sickness and cruelty issuing forth upon the plains and mountains of Europe. . . . Contempt of . . . (the) human nature, weakness, nervous tremblings, fear of day and joy, distrust of man and life, hemiplegia of the will, beset the body burdened and disaffected in its members by its black tyrannous lice.[27]

In contrast to all the frustrated characters in "Dubliners," Stephen later is able to will a change of his condition of life:

> The spectacle of the world in thrall filled him with the fire of courage. He, at least, though living at the farthest remove from the centre of European culture, marooned on an island in the ocean, though inheriting a will broken by doubt and a soul the steadfastness of whose hate became as weak as water in siren arms, would live his own life according to what he recognised as the voice of a new humanity, active, unafraid and unashamed.
>
> He followed his Italian lesson mechanically, feeling the unintermittent deadliness of the atmosphere of the

college in his throat and lungs, obscuring his eyes and obfuscating his brain. The little iron watch on the table had barely passed the half hour: eleven o'clock seemed so far off. He had to open his Machiavelli . . . dull wooden words.[28]

In "A Portrait of the Artist as a Young Man" Joyce takes us directly to the consciousness of his characters, to their voluntary efforts to overcome the deadliness of the atmosphere in which they live. "A Portrait of the Artist" recalls the "Narrative of A. Gordon Pym," for both are studies of emerging consciousness. In both cases the self, in growing with the real, substantial world, pursues the direction of penetrating and destroying that world. Stephen even goes further than Pym in creating the world anew according to his mind's perceptions.

In "A Portrait of the Artist" paralysis sets the general atmosphere, and the protagonists without reasoning accept this paralytic climate of decay just as did Pym or Roderick Usher. Stephen's mind is obscured by the dusk of the outer world. The sensations come toward Stephen, who passively accepts them. "The fellows laughed, but felt that they were a little afraid. In the silence of the soft grey air he heard the cricket bats from here and from there: pok."[29] The image of sensations streaming in to Stephen's ears recalls Pym, who similarly observes and listens to the noises of his surroundings.

In "A Portrait of the Artist" there is a breaking away from paralysis. In the first chapter Stephen, like Pym, states that the "tyranny of home" means squalor and parents. These are both forces that restrain Stephen. He gains the insight that religion and politics are factors destructive of family harmony, personal dignity, and justice. Steadily he seeks by his own effort to find himself. He is angry at being young and being a victim of a world of squalor and insincerity.[30] Stephen has in the last chapter, like Pym, a vision of birds and of a hawklike man,[31] who promise a flight away from all the strings to which Stephen and Pym had been attached since early childhood.

The "Narrative of A. Gordon Pym" and "A Portrait of the Artist" represent in diary entries the final visions. The vision of "A Portrait of the Artist" at the end of the book stands in sharp contrast to the vision of universal paralysis at the end of "Dubliners" and shows at the same time a step of development in comparison with the final image of the mysterious hawklike man at the end of the "Narrative of A. Gordon Pym."

In "Dubliners" the final vision of Gabriel is the universality of paralysis, symbolized by the snow falling indifferently upon all things. Gabriel, as Daiches states, becomes "for the moment not a man different from all other men living in a world of which he alone is the center but a willing part of the general flux of things."[32]

This final image of universal paralysis, the whiteness of snow, is closely related to the final vision of Pym and Peters, who are absorbed by a cataract of whiteness falling on a warm and milky sea. In contrast to this image of paralysis and powerlessness of the protagonists to react, Stephen writes in his diary the night after his talk with Cranly: "Free. Soul free and fancy free. Let the dead bury the dead. Ay. And let the dead marry the dead."[33] Finally Stephen's soul awakens to a consciousness of itself, because it has overcome the nets of tradition and the paralyzing influences of its environment.

In summary, in the discussion above I have shown that the forms of paralysis that Poe and Joyce depict present the following affinities:

1. The protagonists are unable to change by their own will the conditions of the surrounding world. They live in a moral atmosphere from which they are unable to free themselves in their primary stages of development. Paralysis is an integral part of the atmosphere of the stories, and the protagonists accept this paralytic climate without argument. Hence paralysis is in these cases a passivity of volition.

2. Poe and Joyce deal with partial inadequacies of the human being. Joyce terms these partial inadequacies simony and gnomon, referring to the ineffectiveness of either the physical,

mental, or spiritual capacities of the protagonists in the same way as Poe did.

3. Tradition is a bond that paralyzes the development of a city or state. The torpitude of inaction overwhelms the social, religious, and political institutions.

4. Poe and Joyce associate death with the inverted world, the opposite of reason, caused by the paralysis of the will that gives free reign to the subconscious, the irrational. This kind of paralysis leads to the suspension of the normal, rational faculties of thinking and choice.

The Images of Perverseness and Perversion

Some of Poe's and Joyce's protagonists are subjugated by evil impulses without having themselves made the choice that brought on the evil. Their perverse impulses and pleasures in wrongdoing result from a failure to produce harmony within their own personality. Either their will, their reason, or their feelings fail them. The failure of the will stimulates them to *actes gratuits*, the failure of their reason puts them into irrational states of consciousness, the failure of feelings gives them the urge to have "wild sensations." These *actes gratuits*, these states of irrationality, and the urge for "wild sensations" are central themes in Poe's and Joyce's work.

When Poe analyzes the problem of the *acte gratuit* he emphasizes its paradoxical and irrational aspect.

> Induction, *à posteriori*, would have brought phrenology to admit, as an innate and primitive principle of human action, a paradoxical something, which we may call *perverseness*, for want of a more characteristic term. In the sense I intend it, it is, in fact, a *mobile* without motive, a motive not motiviet [*sic*]. Through its promptings we act without comprehensible object; or if this shall be understood as a contradiction in terms, we may so far modify the proposition as to say, that through its promptings we act, for the reason that we should *not*.[34]

Perverseness, according to Poe, is a primitive impulse of the human heart. It is an impulse that overwhelms the protagonist:

> With certain minds, under certain conditions, it becomes absolutely irresistible. I am not more certain that I breathe, than that the assurance of the wrong or error of any action is often the one unconquerable *force* which impels us, and alone impels us to its prosecution. Nor will `this overwhelming tendency to do wrong for the wrong's sake admit of analysis, or resolution into ulterior elements. It is radical, a primitive impulse— elementary.[35]

The images which precipitate violence in Poe's stories are the haunting eyes of an old man ("The Tell-Tale Heart"), the bright, white teeth of a protagonist ("Berenice"), or a sinister cat (Pluto in "Bon-Bon").

Eyes in Poe's stories often play a very direct role in the tales of horror, some stories being entirely based on the "evil eye." Thus the blue, filmy vulture eye of "The Tell-Tale Heart" is the perverse excuse for murder, a perverseness which parallels the early "Berenice." Closely allied hereto is "The Black Cat" in which the cat's eye brings the protagonist the curse of a haunting phantom cat with one fiery eye. Even the eyes of "The Raven," burning into the "bosom's core" of the lover emphasize the pitiless presence of the ineradicable loss, as the red-eyed rats and the demon-eyed walls of heat in "The Pit and the Pendulum" highlight the horror of unsupportable torture. The old captain of the phantom ship in "Ms. Found in a Bottle," with his grey eyes that are sibyls of the future, symbolizes the nature of the entire crew. All these images of evil eyes are associated with images of horror and the evil impulses of the protagonists.

All the rational elements are absent when an impulse of perverseness overcomes the narrator of "The Black Cat," whose driving obsession and anxiety become increasingly intense as the narrative advances. After he has blinded the cat, he hangs the creature as if it were a criminal to be justly executed. However, when he tries to do the same to a second cat that arrives, his wife interferes and therefore he kills her and thus becomes a victim of his impulse to do evil.

The perverse act or *acte gratuit* does not bring any relief to the protagonist, but puts him into a state of uneasiness, as Poe states in "The Imp of the Perverse":

> but in the case of that something which I turn *perverseness*, the desire to be well is not only not aroused, but a strongly antagonistical sentiment exists.[36]

In contrast to these irrational obsessions to kill and to do evil, the protagonist sometimes has the *idée fixe* to carry out perverse actions.

All these acts of violence are natural instincts by which man acts in the way that will entail self-defeat. This self-defeat, according to Poe, originates in any deviation of the normal functions of the will, intellect, and feelings.

Poe introduces the idea of an efficacious, pathological function of evil by means of which the return to a normal state or the original unity becomes possible. This tendency to return to the normal state is, as Poe says, a natural consequence of the Divine Action that he calls "Reaction" or the "principle of Attraction,"[37] and potentially one can find it already in the original unity. The way Poe formulates this tendency to return is described in "Eureka:"

> My general proposition, then, is this: *In the Original Unity of the First Thing lies the Secondary Cause of All things, with the Germ of their Inevitable Annihilation.*[38]
>
> .   .   .   .
>
> Any deviation from normality involves a tendency to return to it. A difference from the normal—from the right—from the just—can be understood as effected only by the overcoming a difficulty; and, if the force which overcomes the difficulty be not infinitely continued, the ineradicable tendency to return will at length be permitted to act for its own satisfaction. On withdrawal of

the force, the tendency acts. This is the principle of reaction as the inevitable consequence of finite action. . . .
Reaction is the return from the condition of *as it is and
ought not to be* into the condition of *as it was, originally,
and therefore ought to be.*[39]

Thus the ontological basis of evil is conceived as a principle of
high tension between the force which strives to multiply itself
(action) and that which strives to return to its original unity (reaction). Normality and destruction are related to one another.
Normality can only be regained under the condition that a certain deviation or anomaly be destroyed.

It is not accidental that one of Poe's and Joyce's favorite images
should be falling and that another should be flying. Every fall
has its responsive flight, every flight its responsive fall. The
longing to fall haunts Poe's and Joyce's protagonists. Pym, following the lead of Peters, is descending the face of a cliff and is
overcome by a *"longing to fall*; a desire, a yearning, a passion
utterly uncontrollable."[40] This longing to fall obsesses Hans
Pfaall and the narrator of "The Gold-Bug." In all Poe's stories of
the sea the protagonists have the giddy apprehension of going
down.

Throughout "The Fall of the House of Usher" there are images
of the fall of the house and of Usher himself. The narrator, like
the house, is falling. There exists a kind of suspended motion.
The house exists on the verge of complete disintegration and
transformation, standing on the brink of a dark lake. The zigzag
fissure in its front points downward into the tarn. Thus the house,
as Feidelson remarks, "is poised between objective reality and
a symbolic status that can be obtained only by its immersion in
the reflecting water and simultaneous dissolution."[41]

In "Morella" the death of Morella is first reflected in her eyes
and is associated with the image of the abyss:

I met the glance of her meaning eyes, and then my soul
sickened and became giddy with the giddiness of one
who gazes downward into some dreary and unfathom-
able abyss.[42]

The longing of the narrator that Morella should die is reflected in nature: "amid the rich October leaves of the forest, a rainbow from the firmament had surely fallen."[43] Like Morella, the rainbow has finally collapsed, and its colors now are broken and fragmentary and will soon be extinguished.

Thus the fall of man is reflected in nature; one can also observe it in the universe that itself is a prey of coming destruction. Thus in "The Conversation of Eiros and Charmion," as Tate points out, Poe "*means* the destruction of the world. It is not only a serious possibility, it is a moral and logical necessity of the condition to which man has perversely brought himself."[44]

This explains why the evildoer not only follows an instinct to do evil but also follows his own instinct to confess the evil deed. The more involved the protagonist is with evil, the more pressing shall be his urge to confess his deeds in repentance. Thereby the link which unites him with his own essence, his own nature, his own character and being becomes more solid and more apparent.

In "The Black Cat" the protagonist is able to justify the murder of his wife. Although the act of killing her brings him instantaneous relief and satisfaction, he is suddenly forced by an inner compulsion to confess his deed to the police. The urge to confess the criminal deed, explains Davidson, referring to "The Black Cat," comes from the evildoer himself.

> The punishment comes not from a church, a law, or even from society: it comes from some inner compulsion of the evil-doer himself who suffers from what Poe otherwise terms "perversity": he must do evil, and yet he wants to be punished and to suffer. Thus he has willed his crime and he wills his retribution.[45]

In "The Tell-Tale Heart" the images of confession are associated with auditory images of hallucinations which lead to the final catastrophe.

> I went down to open it with a light heart,—for what had I *now* to fear? . . . I smiled,—for *what* had I to fear? . . . I bade them search—search *well*. I led them, at

length, to *his* chamber. . . . In the enthusiasm of my confidence, I brought chairs into the room, and desired them *here* to rest from their fatigues, while I myself, in the wild audacity of my perfect triumph, placed my own seat upon the very spot beneath which reposed the corpse of the victim. . . . No doubt I now grew *very* pale;—but I talked more fluently, and with a heightened voice. Yet the sound increased. . . . It was *a low, dull, quick sound—much a sound as a watch makes when enveloped in cotton.* . . . But any thing was better than this agony! Any thing was more tolerable than this derision! I could bear those hypocritical smiles no longer! I felt that I must scream or die! and now—again!— hark! louder! louder! louder! *louder!*

"Villains!" I shrieked, "dissemble no more! I admit the deed!—tear up the planks! here!—it is the beating of his hideous heart!"[46]

This self-defeat is intensified by the association of auditory images with those of deepest remorse. This remorse and the psychological urge to confess the crime by an irresistible compulsion are expressed in irrational terms in "The Imp of the Perverse."

One day, whilst sauntering along the streets, I arrested myself in the act of murmuring, half aloud, these customary syllables. In a fit of petulance, I re-modelled them thus: "I am safe—I am safe—if I be not fool enough to make open confession!" . . . The long imprisoned secret burst forth from my soul.

Then say that I spoke with a distinct enunciation, but with marked emphasis and passionate hurry, as if in dread of interruption before concluding the brief but pregnant sentence that consigned me to the hangman and to hell.[47]

With the inner compulsion to confess, the conscious self of the protagonists does not derive its laws from itself; it does not regard itself in Kant's words as the legislator of the city of ends. It does not accept responsibility and does not create its own values in order to give meaning to the world and to its own life. These characters are dead to the world.

In summary, Poe's images of perverseness that reappear in Joyce's work are images of

(1) the irrational impulses to do evil for the sake of doing evil;
(2) the rational, premeditated forms of perverse impulses or *idées fixes*;
(3) the restless and uncontrolled longing to leave home;
(4) the longing to fall;
(5) the urge to confess and to repent;
(6) the attraction of the abyss;
(7) the principle of attraction and repulsion.

These images, as we shall see, are an integral part of Joyce's work. The melting pot and prototype of these images of perverseness is "An Encounter" that I would like to analyze here thoroughly, since it contains Poe's images of perverseness that are interspersed in all the later creations of Joyce.

Marvin Magalaner explains "An Encounter" in *Joyce: The Man, The Work, The Reputation* that

> the boy narrator . . . seeks in this quest a father . . . though attracted toward the Pigeon-house-Holy Ghost-father symbol, the boys amuse themselves by shooting birds with Mahony's catapult. They succeed only in poisoning the springs from which their desires arise. Instead of a father, a sterile pervert greets them. Their quest fails, for they are unable to reach the house of the Dove, of the father.[48]

This excellent analysis may be extended by pointing out the parallel themes of this account with Poe's themes of perverseness.

The longing to escape is motivated by a feeling of perverseness. Like Pym who has "never experienced a more ardent longing for the wild adventures"[49] the two boys in "An Encounter" are unable to dampen their desire to go to sea. Because they are driven by an impulse of perverseness they see their environment in states of wilderness. The girls they meet and chase are "ragged." When they see the sea, Mahony "said it would be right skit to run away to sea on one of those big ships."[50] Instead of following this impulse, they take a ferryboat; this boat, like Charon's boat, is a symbol for the journey into darkness and oblivion, the symbol of death. They are transported "in the company of two labourers and a little Jew with a bag."[51] The boys, who are driven by dark impulses, perceive their companions and the foreign sailors with a solemn, mysterious and strange feeling: in the green eyes of the foreign sailor they get "some confused notions," yet this pervert reassures them by calling "all right, all right." Their expectations are not fulfilled, since they are tired and have to return and wander slowly into Ringsend. The day seems to them sultry, the streets squalid, and in the grocer's shops they see "musty biscuits" that are "bleaching."

On this way home, Mahony and the narrator of "An Encounter" are completely alone, banished from human society like Pym and Augustus on the Grampus in the open sea. Pym is secreted in the hold of the Grampus with food and drink. Similarly Mahony and the narrator sit at the "ridge of a sloping bank near a wide field, left to jaded thoughts and the crumbs of our provisions. There was nobody but ourselves in the field."[52] The field and the sea are both symbolic images of man's loneliness. In both instances the protagonists are near an abyss, ready to plunge.

The account of "An Encounter" concentrates on the impulsive actions of three persons: Mahony, the pervert, and the narrator whose impulsive life shows common traits with that of Poe's protagonists that we discussed above.

Mahony does not have strength of will to master his perverse impulses. He is indifferent and does not care about reaching the Pigeon House. Instead, he wants to have some fun: "he chased a crowd of ragged girls, brandishing his unloaded catapult."[53] He chases a cat twice that always returns and finally escapes over a wall at which Mahony throws stones. "Desisting from this he began to wander aimlessly."[54] Mahony morally is urged to do evil, acting out of a sudden and blind impulse, without any reasonable motive. Besides this irrational urge to do wrong for the wrong's sake, he wanders aimlessly like "The Man of the Crowd" by Poe.

The pervert with the green eyes whom the boys encounter is a combination of mystification and gratuitous acts, which are the result of diabolic and external impulses. He has a driving impulse, which is later raised to a pitch of sexual excitement and an obsession to whip people, as if he were able to unfold "some elaborate mystery."[55] This pervert has the same urge to do violence as Joe Dillon at the beginning of the story.

The pervert is a madman, since his mind circles through various orbits, repeating the same words over and over again. He leaves and returns in the same motion as the cat comes and disappears and returns or Mahony arrives, leaves, and returns—all three being attracted and repelled as Poe explained this motion of attraction and repulsion in "Eureka." Mahony, the pervert, and the narrator are defined by their attitude toward sex.

The narrator is fascinated by the "unkempt fierce and beautiful girls" of American detective stories. Like Poe's William Wilson he discovers in Leon Dillon traits of his identity, and recognizes that Leon Dillon "awakened one of my consciences."[56] Sitting at the edge of an abyss, the narrator contemplates his own consciousness in the rhythm of departures and returns of Mahony, twice chasing a cat. Like Poe's protagonists he feels the urge to confess and to repent for no obvious reason. As in "The Tell-Tale Heart" by Poe, the images of confession are intensified by images of auditory hallucinations:

> When I reached the top of the slope I turned round and, without looking at him [the pervert], called loudly across the field: "Murphy!" [Mahony] My voice had an accent of forced bravery in it and I was ashamed of my paltry stratagem. I had to call the name again before Mahony saw me and hallooed in answer. How my heart beat as he came running across the field to me! He ran as if to bring me aid. And I was penitent; for in my heart I had always despised him a little.[57]

This quest for penitence is self-defeating. The words of penitence with which the narrator concludes express his loss of hope of finding a father. He is obliged to ask for help not from a superior being for whom he is searching but from Mahony whom he has thought his inferior. In this he is like Pym, who held Dirk Peters his inferior, yet is saved by him. Thus with Poe and Joyce the importance of remorse is functional, since remorse proves that the acts of their protagonists are sinful acts.

All these characters have one principal trait in common, as I have pointed out: they are, in the words of William Wilson's double, "dead to the world." They suffer and are unable, like Pym and Augustus, to have any change of their predetermined condition of life, since they face the occurrences of life that they encounter with complete indifference. This indifference is a perverse inertia that is a major characteristic of Mahony. Mahony does not care about his environment and is just trying to satisfy his own instincts. Most of the other characters depicted in "Dubliners" remain unperturbed by family, church, and state, since they live stimulated and animated by perverse impulses. These impulses make them act like machines. Thus in "Counterparts" the context of the story is mechanism. A kind of mechanism keeps the drinking party in "A Little Cloud" together. There is a pseudo-community of drinking, of sterile emulation, action and reaction.

These mechanical actions are what Poe calls impulses of perverseness. The perverse impulses to whip and beat objects are in Poe's and Joyce's stories similar mechanical actions. In the final poem of "Chamber Music" by Joyce, the image of the whip is assimilated into the rhythms of the final line with its three iambs and three dactyls:

> I hear an army charging upon the land,
> And the thunder of horses plunging, foam about their
>   knees:
> Arrogant, in black armour, behind them stand,
> Disdaining the reins, with fluttering whips, the
>   charioteers.

They cry unto the night their battle-name:
I moan in sleep when I hear afar their whirling laughter.
They cleave the gloom of dreams, a blinding flame,
Clanging, clanging upon the heart as upon an anvil.

They come shaking in triumph their long, green hair:
They come out of the sea and run shouting by the shore.
My heart, have you no wisdom thus to despair?
My love, my love, my love, why have you left me alone?[58]

In "Dubliners" the image of whipping objects or persons reappears in "An Encounter" and concludes "Counterparts." In Chapter I of "A Portrait of the Artist as a Young Man" four pages concentrate on the injustice of a whipping administered by a priest. All these mechanical actions that arise from sadistic impulses separate the individuals from one another. The relationship of the protagonists to their fellow men is also shown by Poe and Joyce in the image of the eye.

Whenever the protagonists in Poe's tales are confronted with an evil eye, they are changed into beings without defense. Frequently, as in "Bon-Bon," they are impelled to follow their dark impulses. Basically, whenever the protagonist is faced with an evil eye, he is a slave. Yet if he looked at the other person with a stronger evil gaze, he would be master of the situation. This is a point that Joyce suggests in the early pages of "A Portrait of the Artist." When Stephen is shivering, trembling and shaking in his bed he observes:

A figure same up the staircase from the hall. He wore the white cloak of a marshal; his face was pale and strange; he held his hand pressed to his side. He looked out of strange eyes at the old servants. They looked at him and saw their master's face and cloak and knew that he had received his death wound. But only the dark was where they looked: only dark silent air. Their master had received his death wound in the battlefield of Prague far away over the sea. He was standing on the field; his hand was pressed to his side: his face was pale and strange and he wore the white cloak of a marshal.

> . . . All the dark was cold and strange. There were pale
> strange faces there, great eyes like carriagelamps. They
> were the ghosts of murderers, the figures of marshals
> who had received their deathwound on the battlefields
> far away over the sea.[59]

The servants, as this image shows, are slaves as long as they depend for their being upon their master, but now, since their master is dead, they make their master's self depend for its being on
their freedom. Stephen, in his anxiety, is overwhelmed by the
dark eyes that he identifies with those of murderers and masters.

The evil eye is an infernal image associated with goatish
creatures:

> Creatures were in the field . . . goatish creatures with
> human faces. . . . The malice of evil glittered in their
> hard eyes. . . . A rictus of cruel malignity lit up greyly
> their old bony faces.[60]

The eyes of these creatures look at Stephen not precisely as
physiological organs, but as subjects, as consciences of evil. Their
gaze seems to ask Stephen something, when he perceives in the
concluding pages of the book:

> A long curving gallery. . . . It is peopled by the images
> of fabulous kings, set in stone. Their hands are folded
> upon their knees in token of weariness and their eyes are
> darkened for the errors of men go up before them for
> ever as dark vapours.
> Strange figures advance as from a cave. They are not
> as tall as men. One does not seem to stand quite apart
> from another. Their faces are phosphorescent, with dark-
> er streaks. They peer at me [Stephen] and their eyes
> seem to ask me something. They do not speak.[61]

With the appearance of these strange figures, the other selves, a
new aspect comes into Stephen's situation. It is an unforeseeable
reverse side of reality which André Gide would call "la part du

diable"; these other selves deprive Stephen by their gaze of his freedom, or at least try to do so.

In "Dubliners" the image of eyes points to the relationship of the protagonist to the persons with whom he has to live and determines again how much separated they live from one another, as do Poe's characters. The gap between the individual and the community is reflected in the motionless gaze of persons whose destiny is solitude. In "Araby" the luminous eyes of a motionless boy stand for stasis that expresses the boy's solitude. The self watches itself see: "gazing up into the darkness I saw myself as a creature driven and derided by vanity; and my eyes burned with anguish and anger."[62] In "Eveline" "her [Eveline's] eyes gave him [the sailor] no sign of love or farewell or recognition."[63] In "A Little Cloud" and "Clay" the final meaning of the stories rests in the eyes; the images are uniformly static:

> Little Chandler felt his cheeks suffused with shame and he stood back out of the lamplight. He listened while the paroxysm of the child's sobbing grew less and less; and tears of remorse started to his eyes.[64]

In "Clay" the static image of the eyes shows that the narrator is finally forced to communicate:

> He [Joe] said that there was no time like the long ago and no music for him like poor old Balfe; . . . and his eyes filled up so much with tears that he could not find what he was looking for and in the end he had to ask his wife to tell him where the corkscrew was.[65]

Poe in "The Spectacles" and Joyce in "A Portrait of the Artist" show that the weakness of the eyes urges the protagonists to confess and to revolt. In "The Spectacles," to take one instance out of several, the weakness of eyes reflects sexual perversion. It symbolizes a revolt against the bourgeois world, a revolt which undermines not only bourgeois institutions but also the basis of feeling itself. The narrator recognizes that he has fallen in love with his great-great-grandmother. His crime was incest.

This incest is a symbol of revolt against bourgeois institutions. The revolt against institutions and especially against priesthood is a main theme in "A Portrait of the Artist." Stephen's weak eyes are the reason of attack by his colleagues. Dante, a fellow student of Stephen, wishes Stephen to be punished by eagles for sexual perversion and says on the second page of the novel:

> Pull out his eyes,
> Apologise,
> Apologise,
> Pull out his eyes.
>
> Apologise,
> Pull out his eyes,
> Pull out his eyes,
> Apologise.[66]

Father Dolan, the pervert priest, administers the whipping of Stephen, because he has broken his eyeglasses and because he has weak eyes, which he considers a crime. In the second chapter, ten pages out of fifty are devoted to a reiteration of the apology theme. Stephen is forced to confess. When in class, Stephen's instructor, M. Tate, forces submission from him regarding the phrasing of a relationship between the creator and the soul, the boys from the class urge Stephen to "confess" his preference for Byron over Tennyson. While Stephen is waiting to play his part, he is taunted by fellow students who ridicule him about a fancied love affair. We have already seen that Stephen is driven restlessly by a sexual impulse, and his plunge is sexual. The plunge has been prepared in early childhood. Although perverted feelings obsess Stephen, he is able to wrench himself free. Thus the plunge is realized by his metaphysical and psychological conflicts; metaphysically he is in conflict with the church, psychologically he has perverted sexual impulses. Although he is close to falling, Stephen, unlike Poe's protagonists, is able to return from the edge of an abyss and not to be enthralled by it.

A reason why Stephen does not fall is that he in time becomes aware of the necessity of freeing himself of all externalities that handicap him in his artistic career. He tries to discover his own nature, that is to say, his character and his being. Yet all he sees is the long monotonous procession of states of mind. Stephen, like Pym, is in a permanent state of suffering, which nothing could increase or diminish. This state corresponds to a sort of psychological tension.

In "Narrative of A. Gordon Pym" and "A Portrait of the Artist" Poe and Joyce represent plastically in images of spoiling food the nagging feeling of guilt that is fretting at the hearts of their protagonists. The food, an external object and the configuration of the intricate material world, could assume a psychic dimension. The material and immaterial world in Poe's and Joyce's work coexist in such balance that one can be read as a precise synecdoche of the other. Thus the word "rotting" in Poe's and Joyce's imagery runs the range from decay and decomposition to putrescence in the material world, paralleling the immaterial one. Pym states:

> Presently feeling an almost ravenous appetite, I bethought myself of the cold mutton, some of which I had eaten just before going to sleep, and found excellent. What was my astonishment in discovering it to be in a state of absolute putrefaction! This circumstance occasioned me great disquietude; for, connecting it with the disorder of mind I experienced upon awakening, I began to suppose that I must have slept for an inordinately long period of time.[67]

A similar state of uneasiness overcomes Stephen in "A Portrait of the Artist" when wine and bread are changed into vinegar and crumble into corruption: Stephen refuses to do homage to vinegar and rotten bread. The Christ of the sacraments becomes for Stephen a malevolent reality. These changes of food arouse in Pym and Stephen sentiments of fear by which they are haunted perpetually.

Over all these images of rottenness in the inorganic world, of crime and perversity in human society, hangs an immense sense of guilt. This sense of guilt is reflected in the images of the fall of man.

The images of the longing to fall and of the fallen being, be it Stephen or Bloom or minor characters in Joyce's work, create another association with the imagery in which Poe's protagonists undergo a vertiginous crisis of fancy to plunge into an abyss. In the first story of "Dubliners," "The Sisters," the longing to plunge into an abyss obsesses Stephen's mind when the lighted square of an upstairs window is studied in anticipation of its eclipse by the darkened blind of the dark room. In "Grace" Joyce considers the weakness of the protagonist's poor fallen nature. Tom Kernam falls in a barroom. He shows absolutely no desire to rise after his fall. It is only through the concerted physical and moral effort of his friends that he is able to get up and to return home. The image of the fall in "Dubliners" reaches its climax in "The Dead" with the oblique falling of snow upon a not so solid, dissolving, and dwindling world.

In "A Portrait of the Artist" Stephen is fallen as long as he is unable to escape the nets of his environment. In chapter four of this novel, Stephen is about to fall, but not yet fallen. In contrast to Pym's *"longing to fall*; a desire, a yearning, a passion utterly uncontrollable"[68] as Pym calls it, Stephen is able to master this desire to fall at the brink of falling, because he is aware and conscious of what might happen to him. This threatening fall is analogously reflected in the vegetable world:

The snares of the world were its ways of sin. He would fall. He had not yet fallen but he would fall silently, in an instant. Not to fall was too hard, too hard: and he felt the silent lapse of his soul, as it would be at some instant to come, falling, falling, but not yet fallen, still unfallen, but about to fall.

He crossed the bridge over the stream of the Tolka, and turned his eyes coldly for an instant towards the faded blue shrine of the Blessed Virgin which stood fowlwise on a pole in the middle of a hamshaped encampment of poor cottages. Then, bending to the left, he followed the lane which led up to his house. The faint sour stink of rotted cabbages came towards him from the kitchen gardens on the rising ground above the river. He smiled to think that it was this disorder, the misrule and confusion of his father's house and the stagnation of vegetable life, which was to win the day in his soul.[69]

Like the house and garden of Usher, where decay possessed every stone, rottenness every plant, so the garden in Joyce's "A Portrait of the Artist" is in stagnation, the house in disorder, "which was to win the day in his [Stephen's] soul." Stephen, like Usher, is on the verge of complete disintegration. The final images that reflect the fall of Stephen, as those of Usher, are images of mental dissolution:

He [Stephen] heard the choir of voices in the kitchen echoed and multiplied through an endless reverberation of the choirs of endless generations of children: and heard in all the echoes an echo also of the recurring note of weariness and pain.[70]

This fall has, like the end of "Narrative of A. Gordon Pym," a responsive flight. Like Pym, who has the vision of a hawklike man, Stephen sees "a hawklike man flying sunward above the sea . . . a symbol of the artist forging anew in his workshop out of the sluggish matter of the earth a new soaring impalpable imperishable being."[71] Images of "wild sensations" open to him then the vision of a new world. One by one Stephen is able to reject all the nets of the environment, such as love and sex, and a flight from all institutions that hold him back to his past open to him ways of escape.

Poe is preoccupied with depicting the flight and fall of the protagonist without any new possibility of escape. Joyce, in distinction to Poe, depicts not only the fallen human being but also the one who is able to become free by the mastery of the environment. Stephen in "A Portrait of the Artist" is about to fall; in *Ulysses* he has fallen. The fallen state approximates the state of death, and Stephen throughout *Ulysses* is struggling toward life again.

The Images of Wild Sensations

"I [Buck Mulligan] remember only ideas and sensations."[72] Sensations are Stephen's points of departure too in exploring this world; in "A Portrait of the Artist" he develops from a bundle of sensations to a matured, self-conscious, dedicated being.

Like Stephen, all children apprehend every object as sensation. He is not interested in objects as things except as they appear to sight and touch. His knowledge of objects, as he remembers it, is by sensation. Later, when Stephen becomes an artist, as though deliberately, he returns to a world of knowledge as it exists before the idea and before the concept, to a world consisting of pure sensations.

This is obviously what happens in Poe's imagery wherein he tries to convey reality. The reality in which Poe's protagonists live appears to them as pure subjectivity, a world of sensation. Their psyche appears to be passive under the compulsion of eye and ear, continually flooding it with new associations, especially with those of wild sensations.

The universe of sensations which Poe's and Joyce's protagonists carry about themselves is singularly personal and unique as well as universal. In their solitude they show that the universe which they are going to write or paint is in themselves. Certain protagonists, laboring under a paralysis of the will to action, do not take hold upon life constructively but allow themselves to be dispersed among the breakwaters of sensations. To others, however, the sensation they experience has a completely different function. It tells them what shape and what color are registered by vision. Finally, there are protagonists whose emotion is tied up to an impression: that of wilderness, splendor, dizzy heights and abysses, instead of perceiving the image as a whole, a mountain as a mountain. The image of the mountain is within the protagonists, and what they express is the response of their own sensibility.

The protagonists of Poe's and Joyce's work perceive the universe in images of "wild sensations." These "wild sensations" suggest the acuteness of their senses. Their visions arise from sadistic impulses or from spiritually motivated impulses. Thus Poe and Joyce show men in the struggle between good and evil. The conflict of good and evil is reflected in action of moral purport and in spiritual aspiration and development.

Poe's "Narrative of A. Gordon Pym" and Joyce's "A Portrait of the Artist" are studies of the emergence and growth of the knowing and thinking self by sensations and spiritual aspirations. Both authors show the development of their protagonists in successive stages of consciousness that depend on sensory impressions which appear almost fragmentary. The minds of their protagonists thereby remain almost completely passive.

A sensation of wilderness, a sixth sense of wild delight, makes possible the spiritual escape out of space and out of time of the protagonists, until then held back by spiritual inertia:

> And now, from the wreck and the chaos of the usual senses, there appeared to have arisen within me a sixth, all perfect. In its exercise I found a wild delight—yet a delight still physical, inasmuch as the understanding in it had no part. Motion in the animal frame had fully ceased.[73]

The sensation of wild delight Poe associates with images of beauty. Beauty is revealed to the protagonist in "Ligeia" when "wild visions, opium-engendered, flitted, shadowlike,"[74] before his eyes; in "The Spectacles" when the narrator compares a lady to the "wildest and most enthusiastic visions;"[75] in "The Assignation" when Marchesa Aphrodite appears in front of the narrator, clustered with diamonds and with wild appealing eyes;[76] in "Eleanora" when she is likened to a "wilderness of dreams."[77]

Whenever the images of wilderness are connected with all kinds of bizarre architecture, they reflect the irrational states of mind of the protagonists. Poe associates these images of wilderness with the architecture of mansions: the ceilings of the mansions Arnheim are "fretted with the wildest and most grotesque specimens of a semi-gothic, semi-druidical device."[78] To Bedloe in "A Tale of the Ragged Mountains" is disclosed a vision of a "wilderness of balconies, of verandas, of minarets, of shrines and fantastically carved oriels."[79] Wilson steals through the "wilderness of narrow passages."[80]

Besides these images of wilderness associated with architecture, there are images of wilderness associated with nature in "The Domain of Arnheim" and with luxuriance in "Landor's Cottage." "Wild shrubbery" is predominant in this account. The narrator of "The Unparalleled Adventure of One Hans Pfaall" speaks of the "wilderness of the ocean"; in "The Gold-Bug" the country is seen as "excessively wild and desolate"; the teeming growth of lilies in the morass of "Silence—A Fable" is alternately termed a "desert" and a "wilderness."

Sometimes the image of wilderness appears in Poe's tales in connection with light. In "The Conversation of Eiros and Charmion" this image of wilderness is associated with apocalyptical light.

Another association of wilderness is reflected in the conflict of good and evil. This conflict is represented by Poe in images of the double. Wilson asks himself if he were not "dying a victim to the horror and the mystery of the wildest of all sublunary visions" and notices that he "grew self-willed, addicted to the wildest caprices" by discovering in his isolation that another boy is also named William Wilson, who is "merely another being in the moral wilderness of Wilson's life."[81]

In comparison with these images of wilderness by Poe, I would like to show the way Joyce conceived them and how far he integrated them into his imagery. Joyce combined images of wilderness with nature. On the basis of their frequency, he seems to present with preference images of the Wild West. The Wild West is the goal of all the restless protagonists who follow their dark impulses to escape from their home for the sake of wild sensations. In "An Encounter" and "The Dead" of "Dubliners" the protagonists escape into the Wild West.

The school boys in "An Encounter" read chronicles of disorder in the Wild West. This image offers them an escape from the dull hours in school. In "The Dead" the pioneers, at the beginning of the story, are trapped in the Wild West. The reader learns

that the Wild West is the goal of escape from Ireland of Gabriel
and his wife, the major protagonists of "The Dead." Gabriel's
aunts and cousins originally lived on Usher's Island, before they
went west. These facts are doubly significant, because they suggest some influence of Poe on Joyce. J. B. Kaye relates Usher's
Island to Poe's "The Fall of the House of Usher"; the critic sees
in the image of the west a hint to Poe's transatlantic country.
Kaye points out that it "suggests not only the decadent house of
Usher, but also the transatlantic origin of Poe."[82]

The image of the Wild West is associated with wild emotions:

> He [Gabriel] felt that they [Gabriel and his wife] had
> escaped from their lives and duties, escaped from home
> and friends and run away together with wild and radi-
> ant hearts to a new adventure.[83]

Another image of wild emotions appears in "A Little Cloud." In
this story a wild trait of character is in the perverse nature of
Ignatius Gallaher. The impression is gathered from the wild and
vulgar features of Gallaher's countenance and character.

The image of wilderness is identical not only with the "wild"
human heart, with the wilderness of the Wild West, but also with
the wild state of nature in general. All these images of wilderness
have one common denominator, an aspect of chaos. This chaotic
state of wilderness is the protagonist's point of departure for
their imaginary trips.

In "Dubliners" and in "A Portrait of the Artist" the protagonists
are at the beginning of the accounts in a "wild garden," a "disordered" room, or a "weedy" garden; or they read "chronicles of
disorder." From this chaos, from the world in total disorder, in
which the protagonists live and about which they read, the protagonists start to reconstruct the images they perceive as their
ideals in their minds. By deduction and intuition they reconstruct
the images of their mind. Thereby certain key images of their
environment stimulate and push them to new sensations and
further investigations.

In "Araby," a story in "Dubliners," the wild back garden is the point of departure for sensational adventures on the imaginary trip of the boy narrator. His environment is in total disorder, in a chaotic state:

> The former tenant of our house, a priest, had died in the back drawing-room. Air, musty from having been long enclosed, hung in all the rooms, and the waste room behind the kitchen was littered with old useless papers. Among these I found a few paper-covered books, the pages of which were curled and damp: *The Abbot*, by Walter Scott, *The Devout Communicant* and *The Memoirs of Vidocq*. I liked the last best because its leaves are yellow. The wild garden behind the house contained a central apple-tree and a few straggling bushes under one of which I found the late tenant's rusty bicycle-pump. He had been a very charitable priest.[84]

The significance of this image of wilderness is the same as that of the disordered room in which Dupin, the major protagonist of Poe's tales of ratiocination, starts his analysis to re-create things in his imagination; he wishes to see things as they really are and not as they seem in reality to a common gaze.

For this reason the boy narrator likes best the detective story, *The Memoirs of Vidocq*, as he explains in the passage quoted above. Vidocq is a detective of Poe's tale of ratiocination. Like a detective he is going to restore another reality which lies behind the appearances. Both protagonists, Dupin and the boy narrator of "Araby," depart from a chaotic state on an imaginary trip in order to find a relationship between reality and the ideal, the seen and the unseen, the perceived and the imagined. Behind these chaotic images of reality in a state of wilderness that actually is only the surface of existence, must lie, as Dupin and Joyce's protagonist think, a presumed reality.

They reveal this ideal reality by recombining the fragmental, chaotic data to an organic whole. In order to perceive this ideal, certain clues are the points from which one sensation after the other arises and leads the protagonists on their imaginary trips. These clues in "Araby" are a central apple tree, a wild garden, silent streets, muddy lanes, dripping gardens, odors of ashpits. In this setting the boy narrator perceives the image of the brown figure, an image that accompanies him wherever he goes. On a dark rainy evening he enters a back drawing room where a priest has died. Through the image that separates reality from the world of his imagination, the image of broken panes, he listens to the rain outdoors. He perceives a light. This light radiates from a distant point, and he associates it with the image of the girl, whose image comes between him and the page he wants to read. Finally, the word "Araby" has a luxuriant effect upon the boy narrator: "The syllables of the word 'Araby' were called to me [the boy narrator] through the silence in which my soul luxuriated and cast an eastern enchantment over me."[85] Therefore, the boy leaves, although in a deserted train, to the enchanted bazaar "Araby." The ideal he perceives is nothing but a very discouraging reality. The bazaar "Araby" is almost empty; and when he walks slowly down the middle of the bazaar, someone begins to turn out the lights. The bazaar is over. The boy discovers himself "driven and derided by vanity."[86]

Thus the perception of the wild garden, the chaotic environment of the boy narrator, at the opening of the story, becomes for him a hallucination; his imagination builds up a bazaar as something splendid and glorious. The reality of wilderness completely disappears for the boy narrator and he plunges into his private reality. In search of his ideal, he transforms the everyday reality of a chaotic world into a hallucinatory world, the only authentic one of the narrator, the experience of which is his final goal.

In "A Portrait of the Artist" this imaginary trip, starting from a disordered world, finds another version of Poe's tale of ratiocination. From an originally simple sensation of a place in wild disorder, Stephen starts his search for Mercedes.

Dublin was a new and complex sensation. Uncle Charles had grown so witless that he could no longer be sent out on errands and the disorder in settling in the new house left Stephen freer than he had been in Blackrock. In the beginning he contented himself with circling

timidly round the neighbouring square or, at most, going half way down one of the side streets: but when he
had made a skeleton map of the city in his mind he followed boldly one of its central lines until he reached the
Custom House. He passed unchallenged among the
docks and along the quays wondering at the multitude
of corks that lay bobbing on the surface of the water in
a thick yellow scum, at the crowds of quay porters and
the rumbling carts and the illdressed bearded police-
man. The vastness and strangeness of the life suggested
to him by the bales of merchandise stocked along the
walls or swung aloft out of the holds of steamers
wakened again in him the unrest which had sent him
wandering in the evening from garden to garden in
search of Mercedes. And amid this new bustling life he
might have fancied himself in another Marseilles. . . .[87]

Stephen is torn from sensation to sensation. These sensations
arouse in him impulses by which the image of this world as he
perceived it first is totally transformed into a hallucinatory
world.

He heard the sob passing loudly down his father's throat
and opened his eyes with a nervous impulse. The sunlight breaking suddenly on his sight turned the sky and
clouds into a fantastic world of sombre masses with lakelike spaces and dark rosy light. His very brain was sick
and powerless. He could scarcely interpret the letters
of the signboards of the shops. By his monstrous way of
life he seemed to have put himself beyond the limits of
reality. Nothing moved him from the world unless he
heard in it an echo of the infuriated cries within him.[88]

The tragic point of this imaginary trip comes when Stephen
finds out that all the sensations make his self nothing but a
bundle or collection of different perceptions without any kind of
substantial unity, identity, or structure, when he moves along

among distorted images of the outer world. A figure
that had seemed to him by day demure and innocent
came towards him by night through the winding dark-

> ness of sleep, her face transfigured by a lecherous cun-
> ning, her eyes bright with brutish joy. Only the morning
> pained him with its dim memory of dark orgiastic riot,
> its keen and humiliating sense of transgression.[89]

In each chapter of "A Portrait of the Artist" Joyce shows that
on Stephen's mind several perceptions successively make their
appearance, pass and repass, and glide away without identity.
He finds out that the perceptions are not experienced as a continuous internally related and unified system of thoughts, feelings, and actions. Instead, the perceptions seem to fall apart into
isolated, unrelated fragments of experience.

> A few moments after he found himself on the stage
> amid the garish gas and the dim scenery, acting before
> the innumerable faces of the void. It surprised him to see
> that the play which he had known at rehearsals for a
> disjointed lifeless thing had suddenly assumed a life of
> its own. It seemed now to play itself, he and his fellow
> actors aiding it with their parts. When the curtain fell
> on the last scene he heard the void filled with applause
> and, through a rift in a side scene, saw the simple body
> before which he had acted magically deformed, the void
> of faces breaking at all points and falling asunder into
> busy groups.
> He left the stage quickly and rid himself of his mum-
> mery and passed out through the chapel into the college
> garden. Now that the play was over his nerves cried for
> some further adventure. He hurried onwards as if to
> overtake it.[90]

As Stephen recognizes on his search for wild adventures that
his perceptions and his self fall apart into isolated, unrelated
parts of experience, he tries to mortify his senses. Only in be-
coming an artist is he able to unify his perceptions and experiences. From the concept of perceptions arises his aesthetic
theory. Stephen makes clear that art is concerned with both ideas

and sensations when he begins his discussion with Cranly. Already in *Stephen Hero* he has begun his essay in defining art as "the human disposition of intelligible or sensible matter for an esthetic end."[91] Thus Stephen considers the ideational and sensory elements of art as inseparable.

Another similarity between Poe's and Joyce's imagery appears in the way they associate images of beauty with wild sensations. In "A Portrait of the Artist" by Joyce and "The Assignation" by Poe, female figures appear as the startling, static images of the narrator's "wild" visions.

In "The Assignation" Marchesa Aphrodite appears as the wild vision of the narrator's mind with "wide appealing eyes."

> Upon the broad black marble flagstones at the entrance of the palace, and a few steps above the water, stood a figure. . . . She stood alone. Her small, bare and silvery feet gleamed in the black mirror of marble beneath her. Her hair, not as yet more than half loosened for the night from its ball-room array, clustered, amid a shower of diamonds, round and round her classical head, in curls like those of the young hyacinth. A snowy-white and gauze-like drapery seemed to be nearly the sole covering to her delicate form; but the mid-summer and midnight air was hot, sullen, and still, and no motion in the statue-like form itself. . . .[92]

Stephen's soul is driven toward a very similar image of beauty when he decided to become an artist:

> An ecstasy of flight made radiant his eyes and wild his breath and tremulous and wild and radiant his windswept limbs . . . a new wild life was singing in his veins. . . . He was alone. He was unheeded, happy, and near to the wild heart of life. He was alone and young and wilful and wildhearted, alone amid a waste of wild air and brackish waters. . . . A girl stood before him in midstream, alone and still, gazing out to sea.[93]

In Chapter V, after the vision of the static figure has reappeared, Stephen perceives that

> the quick light shower had drawn off, tarrying in clusters of diamonds among the shrubs of the quadrangle where an exhalation was breathed forth by the blackened earth. Their trim boots prattled as they stood on the steps of the colonnade. . . . Her heart simple and wilful as a bird's heart?[94]

The last image of simplicity is an image of unity. To this unity, according to Poe's theory in "Eureka," all things return and find their fulfillment.

The association of wild flight and sea reappears in *Ulysses*. It contrasts the image of the abyss:

> He [Kevin Egan] had come nearer the edge of the sea and wet sand slapped his boots. The new air greeted him, harping in wild nerves, wind of wild air of seeds of brightness.[95]

In summary, Poe and Joyce, as we have seen, consider the ideational and sensory elements of art as inseparable. The images of wild sensations stimulate the protagonists to explore the unknown and to be in a "continuous state of flight," although often close to the abyss. They disintegrate their imaginative faculties and separate them from both concrete reality and artistic activity. This disintegration of the imagination can be followed down to the surrealists.

CHAPTER FIVE

The Aesthetics of Poe and Joyce

The Theory of Unity and Effect

In his *Critique of Judgment* Kant added to nineteenth-century aesthetics the corollary ideas that a beautiful work of art is experienced as an end in itself, by an act purely contemplative, disinterested, and free from any reference to desire, will, or the reality and utility of the object. In the nineteenth century these ideas were enthusiastically seized upon and developed by French and English theorists of art for art's sake in their strenuous counter-attack against the demands for truth, morality, and utility in art by philosophical positivists. One of the earliest exponents of "art for art" is Poe, and his successors in this concept were the French symbolists and Joyce.

Considering their works as autonomous entities, Poe and Joyce distinguish two kinds of unity: unity of structure and unity of effect. In the idea of unity of structure they are indebted to Aristotle. As to the unity of effect they are aware how every minor emotion directly arises out of some subordinate detail and does not accept its status as a detached fact in the consciousness of the protagonist. The emotion stresses the unity of the main effect.

In order to produce this effect, Joyce, like the French symbolists, bases his exercise of the mind on strictly calculated methods. We also know that Poe, "as a poet and as a critic of poetry installed calculation, clarity, and consciousness as the reigning values in the poetic enterprise."[1] For the sake of a good composition Poe and Joyce eliminate all the unnecessary narrative elements from their fiction. Their selection and arrangement of the incidents produces an artistically patterned work, a totality in which there is nothing superfluous, in which every detail is artistically as well as biographically relevant.

All-important for Poe and Joyce is the relationship of part to part and each part to the whole. This relationship Poe and Joyce perceive in the universe. The system of the universe presents to Poe a complete mutality of adaptation, a construction whose elements are so fitted to one another that all relations are symmetrical. The mutuality of relation between the world's parts is of the same sort that one feels to exist in the work of an artist who has constructed a perfect plot.

Poe, the artist, explains how he consciously impresses his will or design upon his material. When writing "The Raven," he wishes, as he explains himself, "that no one point in its composition is referable either to accident or intuition."[2]

Since a composition has to be perfectly constructed, Poe compares an aesthetic philosopher with a detective. The aesthetic philosopher achieves through mathematical calculations a unity of plot. This concept leads Poe to the invention of the tale of ratiocination. He proves in "A Philosophy of Composition" that composing a poem is not much different from finding a purloined letter or solving a cryptogram, since the artist like the detective has to establish relationships between data, and the synthesis of the dialectical process comes only at the end. These moments in the dialectical process, when a synthesis is achieved, when certain phrases or sensations or complex experiences suddenly are seen and revealed in a larger whole, Joyce calls epiphanies.

> By an epiphany he [Stephen] meant a sudden spiritual manifestation, whether in the vulgarity of speech or of gesture or in a memorable phase of the mind itself. He believed that it was for the man of letters to record these epiphanies with extreme care, seeing that they themselves are the most delicate and evanescent of moments.[3]

These epiphanies are to be discovered by an aesthetic philosopher or a detective. Stephen thinks, in conversation with Cranly, that if you [Cranly] were an esthetic philosopher you would take note of all my [Stephen's] vagaries because here you have the spectacle of the esthetic instinct in action. The philosophic college should spare a detective for me.[4]

Poe and Joyce assume that the relations of parts to the whole make not only the plot but also the language coherent, a point to be clarified in the second part of this chapter. Both authors are aware of these relationships in plot and language; they suggest in their work imaginary worlds that are made up of elements abstracted from their experience in the real world. Poe and Joyce realize that if parts are separated from the whole they are meaningless. Their purpose and significance are apparent only when the functioning whole is grasped.

On the basis of this relationship of part to part, and of each part to the whole, Joyce tries as early as in "Dubliners" to relate each single particle of the story to the whole. There is less a relationship between part and part than there is between part and the whole.

Poe and Joyce assume that everything in their work should lead to the conclusion. They express in the first sentence of their fiction the idea of the final impression which they wish to produce in the reader. Thus they group their images according to a premeditated design. This design requires a collocation of words for producing the desired effect in the reader. This effect is entirely calculated. The work of art has to be constructed in such a way that one can foresee the final effect. Thanks to this method, artists such as Poe and Joyce can begin their composition at the end and work at any part whenever it is convenient. This Joyce seems to have done in *Finnegans Wake*, according to Joyce's own words to which his friend Budgen refers:

And I remember my old friend August Suter telling me that in the early days of the composition of *Finnegans Wake* Joyce said to him, "I feel like an engineer boring through a mountain from two sides. If my calculations are correct, we shall meet in the middle. If not. . . ."[5]

Poe had taken a hint from the Chinese, "who, in spite of building their houses downwards, have still sense enough *to begin their books at the end*."[6] Another humorous remark by Poe on the subject deals with a journalist, Godwin, who writes his stories backwards:

> Charles Dickens, in a note now lying before me, alluding to an examination I once made of the mechanism of Barnaby Rudge, says—"By the way, are you aware that Godwin wrote his Caleb Williams backwards?"[7]

Critics have observed in the work of Joyce similar tendencies. McLuhan sees an application of this method in Joyce's "Aeolus" episode of Ulysses:

> Poe . . . develops the familiar symbolist doctrine of poem as an art situation which is the formula for a particular effect. The same method of composition in reverse enabled Poe to pioneer the detective story. There is nothing accidental, therefore, about the Aeolus episode being crammed with instances of reversal and reconstruction. Applying the same principle to language yields, in the *Wake*, a reconstruction of all the layers of culture and existence embedded in the present forms of words and speech gesture.[8]

Another critic, William Y. Tindall, also realizes that Joyce had generally a tendency to start his fiction backwards:

> In the works of Joyce, who liked to do things backwards, particulars sometimes precede the traditional images, which, instead of origin, become conclusion. Hidden by the details that embody it, the image is what we must discover and the climax of the tale. "Clay," one of the stories of *Dubliners*, provides an instance of this reversal.[9]

The calculated effect by which Poe and Joyce produced a unity of tone ties their fiction into an organic whole.

Poe and Joyce wrote short stories that can be read in one

session and thus give the reader the unity of impression, the totality of effect, that became one of the major aims of the impressionist painters. The purpose and significance of their work is apparent only when the functioning whole is grasped. The impressionist writers do not adapt their thoughts to the incidents, but, having conceived deliberately and at leisure an effect to be produced, invent the incidents, combine the events most suitable to bring about the desired effect. Poe and Joyce therefore neglect all the narrative elements in their work for the sake of aesthetic devices. They neglect action in order to impress the reader by the aesthetic effect of the story.

Paul Valéry, in "Situation de Baudelaire,"[10] refers to Poe's influence on the aesthetic theories and his psychological effects on the reader, which had some influence on the French symbolists and through them on Joyce. Poe links effect synonymously with impression. In order to produce this impression in the reader, he uses intellectual operations borrowed from the exact sciences and therefore he is able to control this impression by reason.

The effect is a device for a deliberate artistic creation. Poe asks himself the question: "of the innumerable effects, or impressions of which the heart, the intellect or (more generally) the soul is susceptible, which one shall I, on the present occasion, select?"[11] This unity of effect is applied by Poe alike to the poem and to the tale. To him the unity of the work of art is absolute in its origin. Poe saw this and formulated it as the highest kind of aesthetic insight.

To reach this stage of an effect controlled by reason, the "specific" has first to be isolated, in order to be obtained in a pure state. This specific is never the exact description of an object, but the impression that the object makes on Poe or Joyce. This impression they try to transcribe to the reader by suggesting the totality of a mood or impression of feeling. Thus they are able to evoke in the reader parts of their imaginative experience.

Poe discovers how to employ images for illustrating a progression of effect that parallels the movement of the mind. He reduces landscapes to one or two details, showing just the essence of the impression they give him.

> The thick and peculiar mist, or smoke, which distinguishes the Indian summer, and which now hung heavily over all objects, served, no doubt, to deepen the vague impressions which these objects created. . . . In the meantime the morphine had its customary effect— that of enduing all the external world with an intensity of interest. In the quivering of a leaf—in the hue of a blade of grass—in the shape of a trefoil—in the humming of a bee—in the gleaming of a dew-drop—in the breathing of the wind—in the faint odors that came from the forest—there came a whole universe of suggestion—a gay and motley train of rhapsodical and immethodical thought.[12]

In this type of universe of suggestion Stephen lives in "A Portrait of the Artist." The colors, odors, sounds, and sights of his environment make him experience his subjective world. His impressions are conveyed to the reader:

> White roses and red roses: those were beautiful colours to think of. And the cards for first place and third place were beautiful colours too: pink and cream and lavender. Lavender and cream and pink roses were beautiful to think of. Perhaps a wild rose might be like those colours and he remembered the song about the wild rose blossoms on the little green place. But you could not have a green rose. But perhaps somewhere in the world you could.[13]

The reader, as in all the images of Joyce or Poe, has to make his deductions from whatever hints he can perceive in the reported situation of the image. Poe's and Joyce's imagery is presented scrupulously from the point of view of the main character. Joyce tells us what that character sees, hears, understands, says, and thinks.

Thus Poe and Joyce base their aesthetic theories not on description but on suggestion. The meaning of an image is conveyed to the reader by suggestion. Poe, without laying any stress on the ostensible meaning addressed to the intelligence, states that in fiction and poetry there should be an undercurrent of meaning, however indefinite.[14] This undercurrent of meaning Poe expresses in his images; he does not depict things as they are, but the effect that they produce in the observer. This is a commonly used device that Poe gave to the French symbolists and to Joyce.

Mallarmé whom Joyce knew well, as I have said in the introduction, states in 1864 in a letter to Cazalis what he aims at: "Peindre non la chose, mais l'effet qu'elle produit."[15] In 1891 he expresses the same idea again: "Nommer un objet, c'est supprimer les trois quarts de la jouissance du poème qui est faite du bonheur de deviner peu à peu; le suggérer, voilà le but."[16]

The theory that poetry and fiction should not inform but suggest and evoke, not name things but create their atmosphere, is inherent in Joyce's concept of epiphany. The forerunner of the epiphany is Poe who had demanded a suggestive indefiniteness of vague and therefore of spiritual effect.[17] Joyce, following with his epiphanies Poe's method of suggestion in "A Portrait of the Artist" represents, as Irene Hendry points out, the simple faithful by pious sighs and a peasant smell "of air and train and turf and corduroy," or by kneeling forms and whispering voices in the confessional box. Stephen's brothers and sisters are merely voices at the tea table, replying to his questions in pig Latin and singing with "an overtone of weariness behind their frail fresh innocent voices."[18] No clear and full picture of Stephen's relationship with his mother is described. Through conversation we learn that he has had a distressing quarrel with her, in which he tells her that he has lost his faith.

Joyce must have become acquainted with the theory of suggestion "in the short interval between first and last drafts"[19] of "Dubliners" as Magalaner and Kain state. Joyce's work, on the basis of this method of suggestion, grew progressively more obscure from the clarity of his earliest work, *Stephen Hero*, to the half-mysterious word associations of *Finnegans Wake*. In

Ulysses, in order to convey all the mystery that he felt, he reduced his punctuations, made new collocations of words, and sometimes disregarded the rules of syntax. Through the suggestiveness of his language Joyce presents his idea, his picture of the artist in the making. It is how he creates this essential illusion, how he organizes his language, how he makes all the parts respond to the whole, and the whole to the parts, how he creates a totality of effect that decides the artistic value of his work, and enables us to correlate word-painting to the brush strokes on the canvas. Thus fiction is to Joyce, as poetry is to Poe, the supreme act of inventive conjoining, conveying only a suggestive or even ambiguous meaning. Joyce's method of suggestion has been correlated with Mallarmé by Hayman, to whom I refer the reader.[20]

Thus with Poe and Joyce, impressionistic description replaces realistic description. Dujardin points out that the technique of suggestion is the same that the impressionistic painters used:

> Réservant le terme d'impressionnisme à la peinture, on disait plutôt "suggestion" quand il s'agissait de littérature, à la fin du dernier siècle. L'art a pour objet, enseignait Charles Morice, non pas de décrire, mais de suggérer. . . . Poésie suggestive, poésie impressionniste: il y a évidemment une nuance entre les deux expressions.[21]

Suggestion is a psychological device. With this device the beauty of a poem or a piece of prose is not a quality but an effect, a state of mind produced in the reader by a certain collocation of words, phrases and incidents. This principle is a leading device of Joyce in *Dubliners* and *A Portrait of the Artist* as Tindall states:

> The first three stories of *Dubliners* and *A Portrait of the Artist* are presented impressionistically through the consciousness of Stephen, who is made to seem both subject and object. No method could be more appropriate for the creation of an egoist. Matter and method become identical. Telling his story in third person, the author

looks into the head of his central character or observer and records the contents of that head. The author sees external reality only through his observer's eyes, but, since he himself is telling the story, he can select what he wants and ignore the rest. The observer's impressions, selected, arranged, and sometimes commented upon by the author, constitute reality. In *A Portrait of the Artist* we look through Joyce's eyes, looking through the eyes of Stephen, as he looks at himself or sometimes at other things. Our looking is confined to important moments. . . . Through memory and thought the moment acquires levels, meanings and dimensions.[22]

Poe and Joyce use not only impressionistic methods to represent the subject matter. The subject matter is, as in all fiction, carried by the main characters. These main characters are impressionists themselves.

The prototype of Poe's impressionist is Usher; Usher is, as we have seen in the chapter on paralysis, a completely passive personality. All the sensations come toward him and set the mood of decay. Stephen, in "A Portrait of the Artist" is passive. He listens to sounds of things in order to understand their essence; he is attentive to the slightest noises that tell him in a mysterious way of the hidden life of things. This is the attitude of an impressionist poet: passively open to all influences, perceiving a perpetual change of appearances, yet by indirections. Stephen's ego is the reflector of all happenings around himself. He is not yet able to choose his own self.

All the impressions come to Stephen from the outside. The first page of "A Portrait of the Artist" with its magic of words evokes pictures in which Stephen recalls the first sensations of his early childhood. On this very first page impressionism finds its typical application. This beginning is like a poetry of sensation, of evocation, poetry which paints as well as sings. Stephen, like the impressionists, seeks the truth of appearances to the senses, of the visible world to the eyes that see it, and the truth of spiritual things to the spiritual vision. Thus he endeavors after a perfect truth to his impressions.

With this first endeavor we also know that Stephen will become an artist. Stephen has some sort of intuition, a mystic prescience which allows him to perceive supernal beauty. It is in his instinctive groping for supernal beauty that Stephen formulates his aesthetic theories in *Stephen Hero* and "A Portrait of the Artist." In the latter, Stephen explains that he tries

> slowly and humbly and constantly to express, to press out again, from the gross earth or what it brings forth, from sound and shape and colour which are the prison gates of our soul, an image of the beauty we have come to understand—that is art.[23]

Prose is to Stephen the rhythmical creation of beauty.[24] Rhythm or *consonantia* in prose and verse is one of Stephen's requirements of a good piece of art. This idea Stephen expresses in "A Portrait of the Artist":

> Rhythm . . . is the first formal esthetic relation of part to part in any esthetic whole or of an esthetic whole to its part or parts or of any part to the esthetic whole of which it is a part.[25]

Out of this harmony of construction arises, as Joyce assumes in his Paris notebook[26] and in his fiction, a rhythm of beauty.

According to this concept of rhythm, the image which the poet constructs, will in all but the simplest cases be a chain of events, an interaction of rhythms (for a stress undergone or evaded by a syllable is an event). The rhythmical image becomes the objective correlative of an emotion. This is exactly what Poe has achieved in his verse and prose. Poe conveys with his objective correlative the emotion of a rhythmical image to the reader.

Poe produces rhythm by the repetition of words. In "Ulalume" the repetition of words has a hypnotic effect that emphasizes the non-rational state of the speaker's mind. He is in the twilight of the mind where the real and the unreal intermingle and become indistinguishable. It is a point midway between waking and sleeping, between sanity and insanity. This effect produced by the rhythmical repetition of key words reappears in various images of Joyce. Joyce in "Two Gallants" produces a peculiar effect that is not the result of precise observation but of deliberately used hypnosis. Joyce repeats certain key words with a slight alteration of form, like "warm," "grey," "change."

> The grey warm evening of August had descended upon the city and a mild warm air, a memory of summer, circulated in the streets. The streets, shuttered for the repose of Sunday, swarmed with a gaily coloured crowd. Like illumined pearls the lamps shone from the summits of their tall poles upon the living texture below which, changing shape and hue unceasingly, sent up into the warm grey evening air an unchanging, unceasing murmur.[27]

The reptition of key words in Poe's work results in an almost mechanical formalism; in Joyce's it becomes an elaborate arrangement of rhythms and images.

As to Poe, his mechanical formalism is obvious in "The Bells" and "The Raven." Poe conveys the rhythmical movement to the reader, by setting an imaginary image between himself, the writer, and the reader. Images like that of a woman in "To Helen," the dramtic bird and its voice in "The Raven," the castle in "The Fall of the House of Usher," stand between reality and the faculties of the mind or imagination. This method Joyce develops further.

When Stephen tries to make an image accessible to the reader in a rhythmical movement, he considers the relationship between reader, image, and himself, the writer. Stephen sets forth three possibilities: if the artist himself remains the center of emotional gravity, his images will be set forth in immediate relation to himself, and his work will be called lyric; if the artist pauses in meditation, and thus analyzes his reaction as it relates to others, he will produce epic art; if he makes others the center of emotional gravity without explicitly relating them to himself, he will produce a dramatic work.

Always having these possibilities in mind, Joyce transposes his images into rhythms and rhymes. Thus in "A Portrait of the

Artist" Stephen tries to make poems out of images of sight by repeating his visions in rhythms and rhymes. Like Poe he is aware that it is music which most intimately conveys the sense of the psyche's movements.

Poe and Joyce achieve a musical development in their prose that approaches the symphonic in structure. With an interdependence of rhythm, phrase, syntax and words they are able to produce an effect like that of music. With Poe and Joyce the sense of hearing and the sense of sight are almost interchangeable. This effect they produce most adequately and emphatically in the final paragraphs of their work. When the narrator of "The Tell-Tale Heart" is about to admit that he murdered a person, his interior drama is expressed in ever-increasing sounds:

> I talked more fluently, and with a heightened voice. Yet the sound increased—and what could I do? It was *a low, dull, quick sound—much such a sound as a watch makes when enveloped in cotton.* . . . It grew louder— louder—*louder!* . . . I could bear those hypocritical smiles no longer! I felt that I must scream or die!—and now—again!—hark! louder! louder! louder! *louder!*[28]

When Stephen, after his talk with the rector of the school, returns to his fellow students, the movement of his psyche is expressed in the rhythms and cadences of voices:

> He could hear the cries of the fellows on the playgrounds. He broke into a run and, running quicker and quicker, ran across the cinderpath and reached the third line playground, panting.
>
> The fellows had seen him running. They closed round him in a ring, pushing one against another to hear.
> —Tell us! Tell us!
> —What did he say?
> —Did you go in?
> —What did he say?
> —Tell us! Tell us!

He told them what he had said and what the rector had said and, when he had told them, all the fellows flung their caps spinning up into the air and cried:
—Hurroo!
They caught their caps and set them up again spinning skyhigh and cried again:
—Hurroo! Hurroo![29]

The predominant sound effects in this closing paragraph of the first chapter of "A Portrait of the Artist" create a melodious unity. Thus, as the above-quoted texts show, musical effects are for Poe and Joyce the prime quality of prose and poetry. The word "rhythmical" is the core of their definition of beauty.

Poe and Joyce connect the rhythmical creation of beauty with an excitement of the soul. In this excitement they imagine they perceive things of supernal and eternal beauty. There is, Poe believes, an excitement or elevation of the soul in the contemplation of beauty. In this contemplation the musical continuity of the creation of beauty is never broken.

He who shall simply sing, with however glowing enthusiasm, or with however vivid a truth of description, of the sights, and sounds, and odors, and colors, and sentiments, which greet *him* in common with all mankind—he, I say, has yet failed to prove his divine title. . . . We have still a thirst unquenchable, to allay which he has not shown us the crystal springs. This thirst . . . is no mere appreciation of the Beauty before us—but a wild effort to reach the Beauty above. . . . And thus when by Poetry—or when by Music, the most entrancing of the Poetic moods—we find ourselves melted into tears . . . not . . . through excess of pleasure, but through a certain petulant, impatient sorrow at our inability to grasp *now* wholly, here on earth, at once and forever, those divine and rapturous joys of which *through* the poem, or *through* the music, we attain to but brief and indeterminate glimpses.[30]

Joyce expresses a similar concept that the end of art is merely the communication of static aesthetic pleasure through the representation of the beautiful. Art, Stephen tells his friend Lynch, primarily concerns itself with beauty.

> The instant wherein that supreme quality of beauty, the clear radiance of the esthetic image, is apprehended luminously by the mind which has been arrested by its wholeness and fascinated by its harmony is the luminous silent stasis of esthetic pleasure, a spiritual state very like . . . the enchantment of the heart.[31]

For this reason, Poe and Joyce in most instances end their fiction in static images. Thus the rhythmical movement comes to a sudden end in the static image. The final image of denouement both invokes and prolongs the radiance of an aesthetic image. Stasis arrests the mind of the beholder and invites contemplation. In contemplation the reader apprehends sensuously the meaning of the final static image. Poe produces in moments of stasis the sudden spiritual manifestation of the essence of Rowena's being. She is a reincarnation of Ligeia. The moment of the narrator's intrinsic recognition of the essence of Rowena is synthetic and immediate. It is intuitive in its operation.

> And now slowly opened *the eyes* of the figure which stood before me. "Here then, at least," I shrieked aloud, "can I never—can I never be mistaken—these are the full, and the black, and the wild eyes—of my lost love— of the Lady—of the LADY LIGEIA."[32]

The final image of "Metzengerstein" reveals the true nature of the horse that has been in mystical connection with the destruction of the house.

> The fury of the tempest immediately died away, and a dead calm sullenly succeeded. A white flame still enveloped the building like a shroud, and, streaming far away into the quiet atmosphere, shot forth a glare of

preternatural light; while a cloud of smoke settled heavily over the battlements in the distinct colossal figure of—*a horse.*[33]

Wilson recognizes in a sudden glimpse of revelation the identity of his counter-ego:

It was Wilson; but he spoke no longer in a whisper, and I could have fancied that I myself was speaking while he said: *"You have conquered, and I yield. Yet henceforward art thou also dead—dead to the World, to Heaven, and to Hope! In me didst thou exist—and, in my death, see by this image, which is thine own, how utterly thou hast murdered thyself."*[34]

The emotion which the reader experiences with these final static images is an aesthetic emotion wherein the mind is arrested and raised above "desire and loathing."[35]

The static images in Poe's and Joyce's work bring the essential aspects of their fiction to a final unity. The final stasis in their work is an epiphany. The epiphany reconciles classicism of form with the romanticism of experience; the keystone of Poe's and Joyce's whole metaphysics of art lies in the doctrine of final effect or epiphany. Paris points out that:

d'une part, elle [the epiphany] immobilise son objet dans une expression immuable, d'autre part, elle est cette *soudaine manifestation spirituelle,* cette visitation fulgurante dont ont rêvé, de Novalis à Rilke, tous les poètes mystiques.[36]

Joyce's intention as an artist is the clear revelation of the splendor of the intelligible among harmoniously proportioned parts of matter. The final stasis gives brief and indeterminate glimpses of the beautiful. The sudden spiritual manifestations in moments of stasis reveal the relationship of this final image to its parts, since Poe and Joyce construct the whole story in view of this final unifying epiphany.

The effect that Poe and Joyce produce with the setting of the story is epitomized in one object from which an emotional content of associations develops, until finally the epiphany is accomplished. In order to record these epiphanies, Poe had to absorb the situation in the stories in their totality. He cuts out all the meaningless circumstances and reveals at the end, as a unifying effect, a precise detail (in the above-mentioned instances it is the eye, the horse, and the voice) that shows forth the essence of the scene or the soul of the character. Thus Poe's epiphany is an image that is sensuously apprehended. The epiphanic quality is to reveal the significance of the factors that underlie the matter and characterize each tale in turn.

With images of final stasis Joyce achieves, as Poe does, a unity of structure and of effect. In "Araby," "Eveline," "A Little Cloud," and "Clay" the final meaning of the stories is in the static images of eyes; in "Two Gallants" the static image is intensified by a parallel: "Corley halted at the first lamp and stared grimly before him. . . . A small gold coin shone in the palm."[37] This final static image is a circular image toward which the major effect is directed. In "The Dead" the final image is one of motion within stasis, in which the image of paralysis, as expressed in the first paragraph of the book, achieves its epiphany. In "A Portrait of the Artist" the unity of each chapter is epitomized in the final static image that recapitulates the essential relationships of each chapter.

In conclusion, Poe and Joyce are constantly preoccupied with poetic theory which preconceived their work. Their aesthetic theory of prose and poetry is based on the principles of unity of effect and "The Rhythmical Creation of Beauty."[38] As aesthetic philosophers they proceed with the deductive reasoning of detectives. They achieve a rare synthesis of precise mathematical effects and the indefiniteness of music.

In the mathematical order and harmony of music, Poe and Joyce find the necessary control for their imagination. In their work the musical continuity is never broken. The relations of meanings are themselves perpetually similar to relations in harmony. The transition from one impression to another is made with the bewildering rapidity and irregularity of a dream. This is the technique of Debussy and Ravel in music, of Monet and Whistler in painting. They leave as much as possible to the imagination of the beholder, who thus becomes an artist himself, for he must help to create the poem or the piece of prose, or the musical impression, or the picture which is adumbrated for him.

The Power of Words

According to Poe and Joyce, the contemplation of a work of art elevates the soul in moments of stasis and constitutes the climax of aesthetic experiences. The objects that Poe and Joyce contemplate are arrested in space, and their various parts are ascertained simultaneously: the temporal aspects of the narrative give way to spatial examination. This is illustrated by the critic Callahan, who thinks that Joyce commits himself to a type of literature "to be judged in moments of stasis."[39]

The literature of Poe and Joyce indicates relations that not only exist between its parts and the whole, but also within each word, phrase, and paragraph. With language and syntax Poe and Joyce endeavor to create a totally new conception of reality. With this attempt to create a new reality the subject matter has another importance than in traditional literature. The subject matter is important as means; the end is the piece of prose or the poem. The subject exists for the aesthetic reality of the piece of prose or the poem.

In this chapter I would like to illustrate first how Poe conceived this new aesthetic reality created with the evocative power of words and then show to what extent Poe's concept reappears in the work of Joyce. I will not take into account *Finnegans Wake*, since ample research has been done on the evocative power of words in *Finnegans Wake*.

In romantic literature language had not developed into the dry sterile organ which civilization was to create for the exchange of ideas. It was fresh and abundant in images. With Poe and Joyce, as with the rest of the romantic writers, a word contains an incantatory magic. In "The Power of Words" Poe illustrates that words, on the one hand, reveal essences, and, on the other hand, have the power to re-create the physical world. Thus through language Agathos and Oinos are able to move from the illusion that is this sensible world to the fuller perception that is the truer reality beyond.

In "The Power of Words" Agathos reasserts the creative principle of the logos. He conducts Oinos through his realm explaining to Oinos creation and man's part in it: every word is an impulse on the air, a motion produced by thought, whereby dreams are created and a world re-created. Every act, every thought is a creative irradiation of endless consequences into unending space. By moving his hands, Agathos philosophizes, he sets the atmosphere into vibration which engirdles the earth, irradiating consequences in every particle of earth's air. Words are also such creative impulsions, airy and moving incarnations of ethereal thought. He concludes the tour by disclosing a star that he has created in the past. In this final image of the star is manifested Agathos' physical power of words, since Agathos thought it into existence:

> *Agathos.* They *are*!— they *are*! This wild star—it is now three centuries since, with clasped hands, and with streaming eyes, at the feet of my beloved—I spoke it— with a few passionate sentences—into birth. Its brilliant flowers *are* the dearest of all unfulfilled dreams, and its raging volcanoes *are* the passions of the most turbulent and unhallowed of hearts.[40]

Thus entering the pure realm of knowledge, the soul of Agathos discovers its own past active role in nature. This image shows that Agathos is able, like the decadent painters and writers, to make the word the prime agency of revelation.

Poe on another occasion shows that words are not things, but can create another reality. This reality is neither of the mind nor of the things, but a reality of relations between events, images, beings and things.

Tamerlane, the protagonist of Poe's poem, pushes his relationship so far that his "I" denies that the objective reality has any actuality whatsoever. The only meaning to his existence is what he reads into it.

> I have no words—alas!—to tell
> The loveliness of loving well!
>
> .   .   .   .
>
> The letters—with their meaning—melt
> To fantasies—with none.[41]

From this meaninglessness Tamerlane enters into another realm of reality:

> The world, and all it did contain
> In the earth—the air—the sea—
> Its joy—its little lot of pain
> That was new pleasure—the ideal,
> Dim, vanities of dreams by night—
> And dimmer nothings which were real—[42]

Some French symbolists, such as Lautréamont, Rimbaud and Mallarmé, went so far as to believe that language itself can be reality. Mallarmé appreciated the work of Poe especially because Poe tried, in Mallarmé's eyes, to give a pure sense to the words of the tribe. As the critic Camille Mauclair states, "il [Mallarmé] voit avant tout en Poe 'l'ange donnant un sens plus pur aux mots de la tribu,' ce qui fut l'idéal mallarméen lui-même."[43] The whole life of Mallarmé was dedicated to the effort to do something with the language of poetry. He establishes his aesthetics on the incantatory power of words:

> L'oeuvre pure implique la disparition élocutoire du poète, qui cède l'initiative aux mots, par le heurt de leur inégalité mobilisée; ils s'allument de reflets réciproques comme une virtuelle traînée de feux sur des pierreries, remplaçant la respiration perceptible en l'ancien souffle lyrique ou la direction personnelle enthousiaste de la phrase.[44]

With Mallarmé each word has, following Poe's endeavor to renew language, a force of suggestion. For this reason he breaks with the conventional syntax as Joyce did in his later works, in *Ulysses* and *Finnegans Wake.* "Donner un sens plus pur aux mots de la tribu" became the key term of Joyce's aesthetics.

This aesthetic is based on Poe's attempt to build up with the incantatory power of words the total image of a poem or of a piece of prose. Paul Valéry recognizes this attempt:

> Poe had, to an exceptional degree, the feeling for the incantatory element in poetry, of that which may, in the most nearly literal sense, be called "the magic of verse." . . . Its effect is immediate and undeveloping.[45]

With Poe the mental image is a whole, a living unity of form and content, created by words and phrases that appear as images. In "Al Aaraaf" Poe suggests that the poet perceives in silent nature a reality which he deciphers:

> Ours is a world of words: Quiet we call
> "Silence"—which is the merest word of all.
> All Nature speaks, and ev'n ideal things
> Flap shadowy sounds from visionary wings.[46]

To this poem, in addition to all the inspirations from the romantic writers, is related Baudelaire's poem on the correspondences that Joyce knew almost by heart:

> La Nature est un temple où de vivants piliers
> Laissent parfois sortir de confuses paroles;
> L'homme y passe à travers des forêts de symboles
> Qui l'observent avec des regards familiers.[47]

In a similar way Stephen perceives how words are things that he deciphers in nature: "Signatures of all things I am here to read."[48] Thus the task that Stephen assumes is not to express his own feelings or to describe things, but to discover anew the meaning of words.

Poe realizes that we who have become accustomed to reading only with our eyes miss much of the sensuous beauty which resides in the sound of words. For this reason Poe sets the scene in a landscape of his own invention, as he does in "Ulalume." The words he uses evoke in the reader by their sound value a certain effect that disregards their meaning to some extent. In "To Helen," as Cecil Maurice Bowra[49] observes, Poe speaks of the return of Ulysses to Ithaka; not Phaeacian but Nicean barks carry him. Bowra suggests that Poe perhaps had a preference for Nicean to Phaeacian barks for its sounds and the vague echoes which the sound evokes.

Another poem by Poe, "The Bells," has been generally accepted as an experiment in onomatopeia. In each stanza there is a particular set of bells—the silver bells of sledges, the golden wedding bells, the brazen bells and the iron bells of death. Thus Poe tries to convey to the reader by words the mood, texture, and idea of the poem.

Maholy-Nagy reports on Poe's sensitivity to sounds: "Poe once said that 'cellardoor' is the loveliest sounding and most pleasing combination of English words."[50] In his prose and poetry Poe manipulates a variety of sounds. These sounds are integrated with the plot and are an inseparable part of it.

The sonorous envelope of words that Ligeia once pronounced resounds in the narrator's ears; he recalls her passion

> by the almost magical melody, modulation, distinctness, and placidity of her very low voice,—and by the fierce energy . . . of the wild words which she habitually uttered.[51]

The ironic jingling of the bells at the end of "The Cask of Amontillado" is the touch which conveys a particular spirit to the short story, just as the meaning of "the Devil on the Belfry" depends on the sound of the bells in the steeple.

All these sound effects seem to be produced to the detriment of the meaning of words. Therefore passages which are intelligible, such as in "The Bells," show an emotional effect that is based on the irrational association of words to a harmonious whole.

Poe's aim actually is to treat meaningful words as though they were the autonomous notes of a musical construct, capable of being combined without regard to rational denotations. Thus the uttered word of "The Shadow—A Parable" has the power to create a void around itself, to reject all vision coming from the world of the senses and to evoke in the "cadences from syllable to syllable . . . familiar accents of many thousand departed friends."[52]

Words have a psychological impact. With Poe, the French symbolists, and Joyce the word is an entity whose meaning has less effect upon us than the form, color, resonance, the secret affinities of psychic suggestion. The protagonists play with words consciously. Augustus in the "Narrative of A. Gordon Pym" thinks about the meaning of the word blood:

> And "blood," too, that word of all words—so rife at all times with mystery, and suffering, and terror—how trebly full of import did it now appear—how chilly and heavily (disjointed, as it thus was, from any foregoing words to qualify or render it distinct) did its vague syllables fall, amid the deep gloom of my prison, into the innermost recesses of my soul![53]

The effect of the word "blood" is twofold: it is associated with notions of time and space: the syllables fall into the recesses of the author's soul with their always valid meaning. Thus in the image of the word "blood" is inherent a universal meaning of human experience.

Poe gives a clear insight into the rationale of the development of words in "The Gold-Bug," showing that the slightest shift of the position of the letter in relation to the observed "calculus of probability" makes the word something other than it was.

What Pym sees at the South Pole is essentially a dead world in which there are cyphers and hieroglyphics, but no one, least of all the natives, could read them. Only the mind of Augustus can decipher them. Augustus tries to instruct himself on the meaning of the hieroglyphics that reveal to him greater realities than those known to the native.

Thus hieroglyphics and words bring meaning to birth, as Poe shows in his imagery. This concept of the creative power of words became with the French symbolists a leading aesthetic principle. Joyce takes it as a point of departure for further investigations. The endeavor of the French symbolists, who followed closely Poe's "Poetic Principle" and that of Joyce, is to create with the associative power of words a poetry and prose of sensation; a poetry and prose which paints as well as sings. The mere magic of Joyce's words evokes pictures and recalls sensations only for the sake of Beauty. Étienne Gilson observes that Poe's poetic principle, with his ambition to create mere realities with words, had the same end in view as modern painters had thought of as theirs.

> The "poetic principle" invoked by Poe, which he simply calls "a sense of the Beautiful," seems to obey only one law—namely, not to be a mere repetition of the forms, the sounds, the odors of nature as well as of the common feelings with which they inspire all men. When Poe says that "mere repetition is not poetry," he wholly agrees with the conviction expressed by many painters that to initiate new realities, not to repeat already existing ones, is the proper end of the art of painting.[54]

Words, as Poe, the French symbolists and Joyce use them, fix the quintessence of things fleetingly. The words of such characters as Rowena, Little Chandler, Clay, and Eveline are disembodied voices, yet voices of the human soul.

Poe and Joyce attempt to be true to their impressions and intuitions. Therefore they revolt against ready-made impressions, especially against a ready-made language. Stephen in "A Portrait of the Artist" compares the ready-made language with a mirror and the language he creates of his own with a prism. As the young Stephen Dedalus reflects on the nature of language he uses prism and mirror, as contrasting metaphors, the prism for a language many colored and richly storied and the mirror for "a lucid supple periodic prose."[55]

With Poe and Joyce words are not merely color and sound;

they live. Poe and Joyce attempt to match the word with thought, the melody with feeling, to a vital harmony. In "The Raven" and in the "Sirens" episode of *Ulysses* the pure sound "tap" is heard. The rhythmical reappearance of the sound "tap" creates a particular atmosphere and produces a particular state of expectation in our senses. This expectation tends, in some ways, to provoke sensations. In one passage Stephen is journeying to Cork by the night mail. His window is his frame on life, but outside objects flash by with kaleidoscopic effect, only revealing their essence in the repeated and momentary flaring up of tiny grains of fire. Joyce creates wonderfully the impression of blurred images passing before the eyes in total silence by repetition of key words (*flung*) and by his use of the gerund and adjectival particles: thus words take the place of objects, such as *darkening, slipping, passing, glimmering, twinkling*, etc. This blurring of images is an essential part of Joyce's technique—and so often his frame of reference is the window picture-frame. Detail is dispensed with for the sake of atmospheric effect.

> Forms passed this way and that through the dull light. And that was life. The letters of the name of Dublin lay heavily upon his mind, pushing one another surlily hither and thither with slow boorish insistence. His soul was fattening and congealing into a gross grease, plunging ever deeper in its full fear into a sombre threatening dusk, while the body that was his stood, listless and dishonoured, gazing out of darkened eyes, helpless, perturbed and human for a bovine god to stare upon.[56]

Stephen is aware of the harmonious effects of rhythm and color. He achieves a transfer of the senses of sound and sight as Poe realized it in "Al Aaraaf." Stephen, in "A Portrait of the Artist," is extremely sensitive to words. He murmurs the phrase:

> —A day of dappled seaborne clouds.—
> The phrase and the day and the scene harmonised in a chord. Words. Was it their colours? He allowed them to glow and fade, hue after hue: sunrise gold, the russet

and green of apple orchards, azure and waves, the grey-fringed fleece of clouds. No, it was not their colours: it was the poise and balance of the period itself. Did he then love the rhythmic rise and fall of words better than their associations of legend and colour?[57]

In the Cabman's shelter in *Ulysses*, Stephen makes the same transfer between the senses of sound and sight:

> He could hear, of course, all kinds of words changing colour like those crabs about Ringsend in the morning, burrowing quickly into all colours of different sorts of the same sand where they had a home somewhere beneath or seemed to. Then he looked up and saw the eyes that said or didn't say the words the voice he heard said —if you work.[58]

Joyce often makes use of repetitions of the same line or several lines or words, wishing to give words and lines an undercurrent of thought.

> Words? Music? no: It's what's behind.
> Bloom looped, unlooped, noded, disnoded.
> Bloom. Flood of warm jimjam lickitup secretness flowed to flow in music out, in desire, dark to lick flow, invading. Tipping her tepping her tapping her topping her. Tup. Pores to dilate dilating. Tup. The joy the feel the warm the. Tup. To pour o'er sluices pouring gushes. Flood, gush, flow, joygush, tupthrop. Now! Language of love.[59]

These images suggest their meaning by the sonorous effects of words and phrases. Stephen is interested in these sonorous effects of words in early childhood when he starts to create his aesthetic world with the incantatory power of words. On the first page in "Dubliners" the sounds of the words gnomon, paralysis, and simony strike the boy narrator. In "Araby" the boy is thrilled by the evocative sounds of the syllables of this word which "called to me through the silence in which my soul luxuriated and cast an Eastern enchantment over me."[60] Thus the world of the ideal Araby is intensely perceived, since the glare of obvious reality does not outshine their mystic brilliance.

"A Portrait of the Artist" opens in the babbling language and with the irriational viewpoint of a small child. As the narrative develops there is a process of increasing self-consciousness and of increasing consciousness of language. As the child grows older, the language and viewpoint become imperceptibly riper in proportion, until the story ultimately takes the form of the entries which Stephen Dedalus makes in his diary.

A strikingly similar development of self-consciousness and of consciousness of language can be observed in the "Narrative of A. Gordon Pym." Pym develops in successive stages toward a reality which is neither of the mind nor of the things. Davidson in his suggestive study explains:

> It is in direction of this sharp disjunction of thing from idea that Poe was moving in the last pages of Pym: his symbolic white and black, land and sea, barbarian and civilized man are the sharpest distinctions he can make as a means of setting the speculative intelligence apart from what it is speculating on. At the end of the journey Pym is sailing toward that whiteness whose center lies beyond first things and whose nexus may be the creative impulse of the universe itself. Faced with this bewildering and ultimate reduction, Poe can use only a word, an idea of whiteness, the negation of fact and shape.[61]

With Pym's maturity the narrative ends, like "A Portrait of the Artist," in diary entries.

In "A Portrait of the Artist" Stephen glimpses a transcendent world through the evocative power of words. "Words which he did not understand he said over and over to himself till he had learnt them by heart: and through them he had glimpses of the real world about him."[62]

When Stephen reflects on the meaning of words, his anti-social attitudes appear upon reading the word *Foetus* cut in the dark-stained wood:

The sudden legend startled his blood: he seemed to feel the absent students of the college about him and to shrink from their company. A vision of their life, which his father's words had been powerless to evoke, sprang up before him out of the word cut in the desk.[63]

In *Ulysses*, by the seashore, Stephen thinks back to his viking ancestors:

Their blood is in me, their lusts my waves. I moved among them on the frozen Liffey, that I, a changeling, among the sputtering resin fires. I spoke to no-one: none to me.[64]

His social aloofness Stephen expresses in his attitude toward the church:

What had come of the pride of his spirit which had always made him conceive himself as a being apart in every order?
The Reverend Stephen Dedalus, S.J.
His name in that new life leaped into characters before his eyes and to it there followed a mental sensation of an undefined face or colour of a face.[65]

Stephen in *Stephen Hero* assumes an extremely significant attitude toward the meaning of words that most people are unable to read: "People seemed to him strangely ignorant of the value of the words they used so glibly."[66] With open eyes Stephen tries to get the meaning of words from daily impressions.

As he walked thus through the ways of the city he had his ears and eyes ever prompt to receive impressions. It was not only in Skeat that he found words for his treasure house, he found them also haphazard in the shops, on advertisements, in the mouths of the plodding public. He kept repeating them to himself till they lost all instantaneous meaning for him and became wonderful vocables.[67]

This endeavor to grasp the meaning of words is in close keeping with that of the protagonists in Poe's "Gold-Bug" or the "Narrative of A. Gordon Pym." Poe and Joyce illustrate that the secret meaning of a word depends hardly at all upon its objective meaning; it is derived for the most part from the word's sentimental connotation. Stephen, growing more and more conscious of the virtue of words creates with them his aesthetic world.

Poe and Joyce exercise a close selection and arrangement of words, although creating the illusion that there had been no such selection. In "The Raven" and "The Bells" Poe is aware, as the symbolists are, that his is an act of translating into words material that by its evanescence defies verbal description. Joyce, on the other hand, creates out of a maze of correspondences a world, complete and self-subsistent, steadily referring to external things.

Joyce follows Poe's and the French symbolists' belief in the incantatory powers of a piece of prose or poetry. Like Poe and Baudelaire, Joyce associates words and images not according to their usage and pure logic, but their psychological resonance and the mysterious law of universal analogy. Thus Joyce, like his predecessors, looks upon the completed work as a perfect synthesis, all of whose psychic and musical elements have been integrated into an infinitely complex and coherent system of reciprocal relations. Like Valéry and Poe, the Irish writer insists on the intellectual collaboration that is required of any reader of a work of art. Like all the partisans of *poésie pure* and symbolist fiction in France, Joyce maintains that combinations of words take on values apart from their specific meaning and produce a pleasure which has nothing to do with comprehension of the expression. In *Ulysses* the citizens do not express their thoughts through words, but words direct their thoughts. Joyce tries to illustrate in *Ulysses* and *Finnegans Wake* how these words are the concentration of many associations, which vary for each of us in their power of suggestion. Thus in Joyce's later work, words are no longer signs to represent ideas or sentiments; in their combinations they form a purely imaginary substance.

Poe had advanced the notion that melody is the type of artistic realization par excellence because it flows on without clearly defined succession. In a similar way Joyce stresses the musical values in any artistic creation.

We may designate Poe as one of the originators of a climate of linguistic development that the French symbolists elaborated and that reaches its climax with Joyce's *Finnegans Wake*. The aesthetic reality that these partisans of the linguistic movement create is of significance to man's condition at the time, as Tindall thinks:

> The elements of literature have reference, and a literary work is but the semblance of a world. The aesthetic worlds created by Mallarmé and Joyce are forms which, suggesting man's condition, are symbols of living. That is part of their value. "To construct something on which to rejoice," as Eliot puts it in *Ash Wednesday*, is to construct something at once aesthetically autonomous and, by reference or suggestion, moral and human.[68]

In summary, Poe and Joyce convey with the unity of effect a unity of impression. The word becomes for both, Poe and Joyce, the prime agency of revelation. It has the power of suggestion and a full psychological impact.

CHAPTER SIX

James Joyce and the Impressionist and Post-Impressionist Painters

> The true masters do not give lessons, because
> art cannot be taught, but they set examples.
>   Camille Mauclair

Since there appears to be no record of any direct influence on Joyce by impressionist painters, certainly nothing to match the influence exerted on the young Proust by impressionist painters or on Rilke by Rodin and Cézanne, such a subject raises grave difficulties. Any attempt, therefore, to establish parallels between *Dubliners, A Portrait of the Artist,* and the impressionist painters must rest on analogies existing within a common cultural climate in which Joyce, like Proust and the symbolist poets before him, attempted to capture in lyrical prose that elusive magic of the real world which is proportionately less accessible to persons of no great sensibility.

The romanticist Poe and the symbolist group of French writers with whom Joyce was in close contact are aware of correspondences between the arts and also between the senses. All these writers feel that it is possible to bridge the gap between hearing, seeing, tasting, smelling and touching. Baudelaire's sonnet of the correspondences that Joyce knew so well taught that each sensation can evoke every other sensation. A perfume, for example, can evoke the sensation of touch. Baudelaire, perhaps more than anyone else was the father of the new form which symbolism was to take—the subjective interplay of feeling and sensation evoked by colors, forms, smells, and sounds. Therefore, the impressionists

144

also believed they could translate an emotion or a mood from painting into poetry, or *vice versa*, from music into painting, or from poetry into music.

To relate music with poetry is a leading device not only of the French symbolists, of Poe and Joyce, but also of the German romantics and of Berlioz. The devices of these artists are very influential on stream-of-consciousness writing, as the critic Snell points out:

> It is interesting to note . . . that Poe had discovered, in the German *Romantische Schule*, the same theories that were later to be ushered into the world with loud proclamations by the French symbolists. The idea that poetry's largest component and chief beauty was music had been announced by Schleiermacher and Novalis. Novalis wrote, anticipating Mallarmé, who in turn stemmed from Baudelaire, through Poe, that the consummate art should be "poems which sound melodiously and are full of beautiful words, but without any sense or connection." Compare Archibald MacLeish's famous line, "A poem should not mean/But be." Through Rimbaud and Valéry, this romantic asseveration, popularized and proved by Poe in his own poetry, has influenced Joyce and T. S. Eliot. There are, in fact, numerous foreshadowings in Poe of the work done not only by the poets but by Proust and Joyce, including some amazing predictions regarding the "stream of consciousness" and the hypersensory passages in Proust, to be found in *Marginalia*.[1]

Thus the aesthetic principles of their romantic forerunners led Joyce and the impressionist painters to experiment with the translation of moods or images from one medium into another. For example, Debussy could write *"Reflets dans l'Eau"* for the piano, while Monet painted such reflections on canvas. A line from Baudelaire's poem "Harmonie du soir" could suggest the mood for Debussy's "Les sons et les parfums tournent dans l'air du soir." Baudelaire had written elsewhere "Les parfums, les couleurs, et les sons se répondent." In England, Whistler called many of his paintings by musical titles, such as "Nocturne." The symbolists and impressionists spoke of music as "colored hearing," and "as orchestrated verse." Bergson had advanced the notion that melody is the type of artistic realization *par excellence*, because it flows on without clearly defined succession. The whole trend is toward blending and fusion. The result is a fusion of the genres, a mingling of the arts. This kind of fusion, of music and painting, a type of "colored hearing" Joyce represents in the following image:

> He [Gabriel] asked himself what is a woman standing on the stairs in the shadow, listening to distant music, a symbol of. If he were a painter he would paint her in that attitude. Her blue felt hat would show off the bronze of her hair against the darkness and the dark panels of her skirt would show off the light ones. *Distant Music* he would call the picture if he were a painter.[2]

This imagery is pictorial. Joyce and the impressionists, among them Poe, show a kaleidoscopic view of life. They try to cast new lights and shadows on life but without thereby deciphering it. Although the impressionists first of all take only the life of the senses into account, they seek something underneath the appearances, some plastic symbol which shall be more significant of reality than the exact reproduction can be. Thus the impressionist sculptors record accurately their visual sensations and reveal thereby an undercurrent of meaning. Budgen points out that Rodin considered the

> visible in the human body as a fraction of that which lies below the surface. . . . As with the human body at rest, so with the human being in action. What a man does is only a part, and that the smaller part of his character. What he thinks and dreams is the greater part.[3]

Joyce in his early work takes only life into account, the life of the senses. With the impressionists he does not see country houses with the eyes of an architect, but rather as Poe sees the

House of Usher, concentrating on its surrounding atmosphere. Like Poe, he expresses the soul of these houses by the atmospheric conditions which surround them. The impressionists discover in the atmospheric haziness a particular climate of morning and evening, spring and autumn, a climate which corresponds with the psyche of what they describe. Thus it seems to Stephen in *Stephen Hero* that "the damp Dublin winter seemed to harmonize with his inward sense of unreadiness."[4]

With the creation of atmosphere a new concept of beauty arises. This was realized by Poe and had a strong influence on English impressionists: When the English painter Sickert was asked what an impressionist was, he answered:

> To attempt anything like an exposition of the aims of painters so varied in their intentions as the present group, would be a difficult task. . . . Essentially and firstly it is not realism. It has no wish to record anything merely because it exists. It is not occupied in a struggle to make intensely real and solid the sordid or superficial details of the subject it selects. It accepts, as the aim of the picture, what Edgar Allan Poe asserts to be the sole legitimate province of the poem, *beauty*. In its search through visible nature for the elements of this same beauty, it does not admit the narrow interpretation of the word "Nature" which would stop short outside the four-mile radius.[5]

This search to present beauty in art leads Stephen to a discussion of plastic and pictorial art. In this discussion, as expounded in *Stephen Hero* and "A Portrait of the Artist" Stephen clarifies the aim of modern art. Stephen openly attacks Lessing's distinction in *Laocoön* or of the *Limits of Painting and Poetry*.

> The treatises [on Laocoön] which were recommended to him he found valueless and trifling; the Laocoön of Lessing irritated him. He wondered how the world could accept as valuable contributions such (fantas) fanciful generalisations. What finer certitude could be attained by the artist if he believed that ancient art was plastic and that modern art was pictorial. . . .[6]

Thus Stephen does not agree with Lessing's statement in *Laocoön* that painting and sculpture are limited in time and space, hence static, whereas poetry is exclusively related to a realization of sequence in time, hence dynamic and narrative. Lessing thinks that each category of art, consequently, implies a different set of values. Stephen refutes such generalizations and suggests that the aesthetic image is that beauty which has the three attributes of integrity, *consonantia*, and clarity. To Stephen the first stage of human apprehension is the distinguishing and organizing of sense impressions by the sensitive soul, the apprehension of the object as a sensible thing. To Stephen the image presents itself as a sheer visual form instead of a locally and practically related object. Stephen apprehends the image "as *one* thing . . . self-bounded and self-contained upon the immeasurable background of space or time which is not it."[7] This image is to Joyce and to the impressionist painters not a product of the intellect except in so far as intellect is involved in that creative operation of the whole mind. Stephen explains that if we conceive a basket as a completely visual thing, then we abstract its appearance from its material existence.[8] What we see in this way becomes simply a thing of vision—a form, an image. It detaches itself from the actual setting and acquires a different context. A novel, a poem or a story is to Stephen a fully developed image, including many minor and subordinate images. These images are represented differently in lyrical, epical and dramatic art. In lyrical art the aesthetic image is presented by the artist in immediate relation to himself, and may be rendered by a fleeting emotion or moment of pure feeling. In epical art, the image is presented in mediate relation to the artist and his audience; the "center of emotional gravity"[9] is equidistant between the two. In dramatic art, the image is presented in immediate relation to others; the artistic personality refines itself "out of existence."[10] Thus the sensible aspect of the object is transformed by the mind so that it may become capable of conceptual apprehension of the object as a sensible thing.

If we follow Stephen's development in "A Portrait of the Artist" we see that the spirit of beauty is revealed to him hazily in sounds. Some of his earliest memories are fused in one common apprehension:

> The bell rang for night prayers and he filed out of the study hall after the others and down the staircase and along the corridors to the chapel. The corridors were darkly lit and the chapel was darkly lit. Soon all would be dark and sleeping. There was cold night air in the chapel and the marbles were the colour the sea was at night. The sea was cold day and night: but it was colder at night. It was cold and dark under the seawall beside his father's house. But the kettle would be on the hob to make punch.[11]

Stephen indirectly enjoys shapes and colors, sounds and tactile feelings, taste and smell since these take their quality from the words by the means of which they are transmitted. Then Stephen's aesthetic emotions become spiritualized and from his concrete impressions of beauty emerges a vague feeling of a general essence or spirit of Beauty. Thus the end of art to Stephen is the attainment of a formal purity and aesthetic perfection.

As stated in the previous chapter, Poe and the French symbolists try to evoke unmentioned objects with illusive words. Stephen, following this tradition, is mostly concerned with the things not seen, but "reflected through the prism of a language many-coloured and richly storied."[12] Accordingly, the evocation of a mood or a revery is to Stephen the distinctive value of his language.

In some passages Joyce sacrifices sense to sound in order that the elements of pitch and duration might aid in creating the effect. For the sake of this effect Joyce with the impressionists revolts against a ready-made language and against the bondage of traditional form. What the painters did with colors Joyce achieves with words: a rhythm of vague, intangible and evanescent effects:

> First came the vacation and then the next term and then
> vacation again and then again another term and then
> again the vacation. It was like a train going in and out
> of tunnels and that was like the noise of the boys eating
> in the refectory when you opened and closed the flaps of
> the ears. Term, vacation; tunnel, out; noise, stop. How
> far away it was![13]

The dissociation of sound and sense, recommended by the impressionist writers, parallel with the dissociation of colors, recommended by the impressionist painters, entered a good deal into the notion of epiphany. Joyce observes the fleeting "sudden spiritual manifestation, whether in the vulgarity of speech or of gesture or in a memorable phase of the mind itself"[14] which his ears perceive in daily life. This Joyce illustrates in "Dubliners." The protagonists are unable to enter directly into the thought of their fellow men, but realize the meaning of exterior facts in which inner qualities show forth. By recording these outer experiences Joyce produces a kind of epiphany in psychological transposition. The epiphany reveals a reality that shows forth from exterior details: thus the word "foetus" carved in a school desk, suddenly focuses for Stephen "his monstrous way of life."[15]

Just as Joyce tries to weave across his prose the pure sense of words, thus the impressionist painters seek to weave across their canvas the unbroken weft of color. The impressionist painters catch the fugitive aspects of their subject and reveal faithfully nature as seen through their temperaments. This principle then beholds in nature a means rather than an end. Joyce, like these impressionist painters, takes thereby only parts of life into account: the life of the senses or that of the soul, by expressing the vital forms with which they are animated.

Thereby a certain effect is produced with the arrangement of colors, light, and shade on a pictorial plane. Stephen explains the interdependence of color and light in *Ulysses*:

Colours depend on the light you see. Stare the sun for example like the eagle then look at a shoe see a blotch blob yellowish. Wants to stamp his trademark on everything. Instance, that cat this morning on the staircase. Colour of brown turf. Say you never see them with three colours. Not true. That half tabbywhite tortoiseshell in the *City Arms* with the letter em on her forehead. Body fifty different colours. Howth a while ago amethyst. Glass flashing.[16]

Stephen believes with the impressionist painters that there is no color peculiar to any object, but only more or less rapid vibration of light upon its surface. Sensations are caused by light. The impressionists record their visual sensations and observe how color fuses into color. This Bloom perceives:

Evening hours, girls in grey gauze. Night hours then black with daggers and eyemasks. Poetical idea pink, then golden, then grey, then black. Still true to life also. Day, then night.[17]

Shadow or darkness are to the impressionists not the absence of light outdoors, but only a different-colored light. For Joyce light is the sole source of color. And colors, connected with images of sounds are in themselves capable of creating forms and contours, as Joyce suggests in "After the Race": "They drove by the crowd, blended now into soft colours, to a music of merry bells."[18]

Black has disappeared from the impressionist painters' palette. It is the prismatic colors alone that create the lights and shadows and become the substance of the form. Thus objects are seen as colored shapes that one perceives only because they are colored. These shapes and colors the impressionists perceive relatively. Far from being fixed conditions, they are continually modified by lighting and atmosphere. This we can observe in an image of "A Portrait of the Artist," when Stephen is in the college at Clongowes. Stephen first sees his fellow students in red, blue and yellow, because his eye receives certain vibrations. The deeper he indulges in reveries, however, the more the colors he perceives fade into greyish tones:

> It seemed to him a solemn time: and he wondered if that was the time when the fellows in Clongowes wore blue coats with brass buttons and yellow waistcoats and caps of rabbitskin and drank beer like grownup people and kept greyhounds of their own to course the hares with.
>
> He looked at the window and saw that the daylight had grown weaker. There would be cloudy grey light over the playgrounds. There was no noise on the playgrounds.[19]

Another image illustrates that the entire composition is conditioned. The atmosphere of a gay and warm September day hovers over a generalized, loosely defined crowd with no sharp lines. The contrasts of color are substituted by fusions of light and shadow. Perspective is completely lacking. The surface effect is predominant, and the effect of depth is absent. Any severe geometric areas are sacrificed to tonal diffusion. The image might be compared with Pissarro's city impressions and Renoir's "Pont Neuf."

> The grey warm evening of August had descended upon the city and a mild warm air, a memory of summer, circulated in the streets. The streets, shuttered for the repose of Sunday, swarmed with a gaily coloured crowd. Like illumined pearls the lamps shone from the summits of their tall poles upon the living texture below which, changing shape and hue unceasingly, sent up into the warm grey evening air an unchanging, unceasing murmur.[20]

In other images the rhythm of music blurs all the definite outlines of thought. Although, as we can see in the following image, there is no color peculiar to any object, the infinity of atmospheric life is dense. It parallels Stephen's unrest:

He passed out of the schoolhouse and halted under the shed that flanked the garden. From the theatre opposite came the muffled noise of the audience and sudden brazen clashes of the soldiers' band. The light spread upwards from the glass roof making the theatre seem a festive ark, anchored among the hulks of houses, her frail cables of lanterns looping her to her moorings. A sidedoor of the theatre opened suddenly and a shaft of light flew across the grassplots. A sudden burst of music issued from the ark, the prelude of a waltz: and when the sidedoor closed again the listener could hear the faint rhythm of music. The sentiment of the opening bars, their languor and supple movement, evoked the incommunicable emotion which had been the cause of all his day's unrest and of a moment before.[21]

Similarly, in the "Circe" episode the more or less dense atmosphere is significant. Joyce evokes with musical accompaniment various atmospheres of intoxication and hallucination that are appropriate to the appearance of kings and the transient mobs of strangers.

Joyce attempts, as the impressionist musicians and painters do, to suggest the atmosphere of drowsiness and dreaminess. In order to evoke this kind of atmosphere, both Debussy and Monet are drawn especially to clouds, waves, ripples in water, and the foliage in woods and gardens. Joyce works with similar devices, since he feels that by suggestion, by mysterious images rich in symbolic associations, a particular effect or impression might be produced in the reader. Thus when Stephen opens a book about Holland, a strange feeling of happiness overcomes him in a wave-like movement:

There was a book in the library about Holland. There were lovely foreign names in it and pictures of strange-looking cities and ships. It made you feel so happy.

How pale the light was at the window! But that was nice. The fire rose and fell on the wall. It was like waves. Someone had put coal on and he had heard voices. They were talking. It was the noise of the waves.

Or the waves were talking among themselves as they rose and fell.

He saw the sea of waves, long dark waves rising and falling, dark under the moonless night. A tiny light twinkled at the pierhead where the ship was entering: and he saw a multitude of people gathered by the waters' edge to see the ship that was entering their harbour. A tall man stood on the deck, looking out towards the flat dark land.[22]

This image is visual, vague, and audible. The repetition of key nouns is significant. It adds to intensify and to transfigure the boat into a strange, drowsy vision. The audible effects replace the impressionistic device of blurred colors and sights.

Joyce tries, following the example of the impressionists, to render the climate of the modern city. He conceives it like the painter Monet, suggesting its silhouettes or some of its representative buildings in rain or mist, sunshine or darkness. Joyce evokes thereby the soul instead of the architecture of the city. Vague *états d'âme* are his chief interest. What Monet represents with "Impression: Sunrise" Joyce depicts in words:

A veiled sunlight lit up faintly the grey sheet of water where the river was embayed. In the distance along the course of the slowflowing Liffey slender masts flecked the sky and, more distant still, the dim fabric of the city lay prone in haze. Like a scene on some vague arras, old as man's weariness, the image of the seventh city of christendom was visible to him across the timeless air, no older nor more weary nor less patient of subjection than in the days of the thingmote.[23]

With the newly created atmosphere a new concept of space arises; space is conceived no longer as a geometrical medium of perspective. The representation of space, not articulated, without precise planes, unites nearness and distance. There is a continuous atmospheric impression, created without any tactile values:

Disheartened, he [Stephen] raised his eyes towards the slowdrifting clouds, dappled and seaborne. They were voyaging across the deserts of the sky, a host of nomads on the march, voyaging high over Ireland, westward bound. The Europe they had come from lay out there beyond the Irish Sea, Europe of strange tongues and valleyed and woodbegirt and citadelled and of entrenched and marshalled races. He heard a confused music within him as of memories and names which he was almost conscious of but could not capture even for an instant; then the music seemed to recede, to recede, to recede: and from each receding trail of nebulous music there fell always one long-drawn calling note, piercing like a star the dusk of silence.[24]

In other instances, Joyce creates space by means of a juxtaposition of colors: these are equally dense. In the following image of a still-life, Joyce does not render depth, but atmosphere; the colors of the flame, holly, and ivy evoke the texture of Stephen's mind:

But Clongowes was far away: and the warm heavy smell of turkey and ham and celery rose from the plates and dishes and the great fire was banked high and red in the grate and the green ivy and red holly made you feel so happy and when dinner was ended the big plum pudding would be carried in, studded with peeled almonds and sprigs of holly, with bluish fire running around it and a little green flag flying from the top.[25]

Thus space is no more a geometrical medium, but a medium of light which the painter can render by color. The qualities of form and space are nowhere apparent. Sometimes, however, forms appear that are inferred from the different intensities of light reflected from the surfaces. Thus space is synonymous with matter or externality:

The forms of the community emerged from the gust-blown vestments, the dean of studies, the portly florid bursar with his cap of grey hair, the president, the little

priest with featherly hair who wrote devout verses, the
squat peasant form of the professor of economics, the
tall form of the young professor of mental science discussing on the landing a case of conscience . . . the
plump roundheaded professor of Italian.[26]

As space is implied in the change of hue that color undergoes
in passing through atmosphere, space, accordingly, is implied
in the change of sounds. These, by repetition create an atmosphere and change the meaning of words. Stephen, when thinking of red and green roses, repeats to himself different colors and
listens to the sounds of these words. These words undergo a
change and he gathers finally the impression that there were
somewhere in the world green roses.

White roses and red roses: those were beautiful colours
to think of. And the cards for first place and third place
were beautiful colours too: pink and cream and lavender. Lavender and cream and pink roses were beautiful
to think of. Perhaps a wild rose might be like those
colours and he remembered the song about the wild
rose blossoms on the little green place. But you could
not have a green rose. But perhaps somewhere in the
world you could.[27]

The way Stephen disperses his visual impressions of red and
green roses into a multiplicity of colored dots shows that he tries
to break reality up into elusive, impalpable fragments. With the
breaking up of reality into fragments, Joyce and the impressionist painters observe the play of sunlight on objects through an
envelope of atmosphere. Thus sunlight under which Stephen
describes a breakfast table is split up prismwise. Stephen perceives the breakfast food as broken streaks, morsels, crusts,
bread. Joyce evokes the impression of brokenness as effectively
as a painter does it with dots of color: forms disappear in atmosphere, light becomes iridescent and solidity fails:

It was a bright Sunday morning of early summer, prom-
ising heat, but with a fresh breeze blowing. All the
windows of the boarding house were open and the lace

curtains ballooned gently towards the street beneath
the raised sashes. The belfry of George's Church sent
out constant peals and worshippers, singly or in groups,
traversed the little circus before the church, revealing
their purpose by their self-contained demeanor no less
than by the little volumes in their gloved hands. Breakfast was over in the boarding house and the table of the
breakfast-room was covered with plates on which lay
yellow streaks of eggs with morsels of bacon-fat and
bacon-rind. Mrs. Mooney sat in the straw arm-chair
and watched the servant Mary remove the breakfast
things. She made Mary collect the crusts and pieces of
broken bread to help to make Tuesday's bread pudding.[28]

Thus Joyce reproduces through the repetition of key words the
same effect that painters achieve with colored dots. Nouns pre-
dominate in these images. The nouns are color spots without any
verbal harmonization.

Joyce has the insight that in order to represent life as it really
is, it must be broken down into its fleeting transitory states.
Thereby the human elements lose their autonomous superiority
in his work. As the impressionist painters depicted only the
passing moments in nature, so of all moments they preferred
the most passive and unconcerned, without trace of will or
strain. Accordingly, Joyce in "After the Race" describes a group
of young people. Their gestures seem to be stiff, empty and unnatural, although, obviously, the group seems gay. Each person
of the group is an actor. Their significant gestures seem to be as
artificial as the city through which they stroll:

That night the city wore the mask of a capital. The five
young men strolled along Stephen's Green in a faint
cloud of aromatic smoke. They talked loudly and gaily
and their cloaks dangled from their shoulders. The people made way for them. . . . They drove by the crowd,
blended now into soft colours, to a music of merry
bells.[29]

Although these five young men seem to celebrate the victory of a race, they exhibit themselves and are the clowns of their own actions. These personalities resemble emptied statues of a drama. The action preserves the traits of the inhuman and emptied expressions of the young people. They live in their own hell and each only thinks of his own sake, until they are made aware of reality by the admonition: "Daybreak, gentlemen!"[30]

The impressionists break life into its fleeting, transitory aspects. Accordingly, they divide up their vision of nature corresponding to the effects of sun, mist, and dusk. These effects have psychological impact on the characters. The weak, almost disembodied Little Chandler has the same melancholic appearance or "look" as the veil of melancholy that hovers over all nature with sunset, when life is dying.

> His hands were white and small, his frame was fragile, his voice was quiet and his manners were refined. . . . The glow of late autumn sunset covered the grass plots and walks. It cast a shower of kindly golden dust on the untidy nurses and decrepit old men who drowsed on the benches; it flickered upon all the moving figures—on the children who ran screaming . . . he became sad. . . . The golden sunset was waning and the air had grown sharp. A horde of grimy children populated the street. . . . As he crossed Grattan Bridge he looked down the river towards the lower quays and pitied the poor stunted houses. They seemed to him a band of tramps, huddled together along the riverbanks, their old coats covered with dust and soot, stupefied by the panorama of sunset and waiting for the first chill of night to bid them arise. . . . There were so many different moods and impressions that he wished to express in verse.[31]

Portraits are immersed in a luminous fluid of colors. There is no feature that would describe the man's character. Color applied in formless patches, as in the following image, supplies the modelling, and the total effect is arrived at through a general restlessness that hovers all over the portrait.

He [Gabriel] was a stout, tallish young man. The high colour of his cheeks pushed upwards even to his forehead, where it scattered itself in a few formless patches of pale red; and on his hairless face there scintillated restlessly the polished lenses and the bright gilt rims of the glasses which screened his delicate and restless eyes.[32]

The impressionists try to render the fleeting moments of experience. In *Ulysses*, however, Joyce depicts only the present time and place of the times and places that are passing, in a rapid flux of images: "Hold to the now, the here, through which all the future plunges to the past."[33] The painter Budgen says that Joyce is most successful in the superimposition of images, representing time and space in a new way:

Joyce with his own material can do what no painter can do within the limits of color and a flat surface. He can build up his picture out of many superimposed planes of time, so that any one of his persons can give any number of impersonations.[34]

As we have seen in "A Portrait of the Artist" the representation of space, not articulated and without precise planes, unites nearness and distance. Yet in *Ulysses* Joyce evokes a new conception of space, a kind of flat perspective that might be compared with the paintings of Cézanne. Cézanne launched a notion of flat painting that Seurat describes as the "art of hollowing out a surface." Cézanne is not satisfied with arbitrary impressions on the retina at a certain time and on a certain place, with appearances as the impressionist painters accepted them. Cézanne points to the defects of impressionism which had as its exclusive concern problems of illumination. These had caused the loss of plastic form, of decorative pattern and of design in painting. Thus Cézanne formulated the ideas which led logically to cubism and eventually to pure abstractionism. Joyce produces in *Ulysses* the new type of flat perspective with an interplay of colors:

> Signs on a white field. Somewhere to someone in your flutiest voice. The good bishop of Cloyne took the veil of the temple out of his shovel hat: veil of space with coloured emblems hatched on its field. Hold hard. Coloured on a flat: yes, that's right. Flat I see, then think distance, near, far, flat I see, east, back. Ah, see now. Falls back suddenly, frozen in stereoscope. Click does the trick. You find my words dark. Darkness is in our souls, do you not think? Flutier. Our souls, shame-wounded by our sins, cling to us yet more, a woman to her lover clinging, the more the more.[35]

Cézanne perceives behind the appearances of forms a hidden reality, behind the contingent an essential reality. Forms to Cézanne are only the exterior aspect of an idea. The primordial idea is the soul of things. Thus a landscape, a few apples on a plate, an arrangement of abstract forms is pictorial in its effect. The spiritual quality of the image is intrinsic in the design of the particular work itself.

A still life by Joyce gives this impression. The objects are set on the table in a rhythmical order. Joyce evokes in this image the essential geometry of natural forms. Solid objects are put on the far ends of parallel lines. These parallel lines seem to bring the distant solid forms closer into the foreground. The colors red, yellow, green intensify the forms of the objects. Thus Joyce modulates with color; color constructs the form and sets the rhythm of the picture. The geometrization of this still life resides in the forms of the square, the pyramid, the rectangle and other forms that are comparable to the cylinder, the cone and the sphere, forms which construct the aesthetic design:

> A fat brown goose lay at one end of the table and at the other end, on a bed of creased paper strewn with sprigs of parsley, lay a great ham, stripped of its outer skin and peppered over with crust crumbs, a neat paper frill round its shin and beside this was a round of spiced

beef. Between these rival ends ran parallel lines of side-dishes: two little minsters of jelly, red and yellow; a shallow dish full of blocks of blancmange and red jam, a large green leaf-shaped dish with a stalk-shaped handle, on which lay bunches of purple raisins and peeled almonds, a companion dish on which lay a solid rectangle of Smyrna figs, a dish of custard topped with grated nutmeg, a small bowl full of chocolates and sweets wrapped in gold and silver papers and a glass vase in which stood some tall celery stalks. In the centre of the table there stood, as sentries to a fruit-stand which upheld a pyramid of oranges and American apples, two squat old-fashioned decanters of cut glass, one containing port and the other dark sherry. On the closed square piano a pudding in a huge yellow dish lay in waiting and behind it were three squads of bottles of stout and ale and minerals, drawn up according to the colours of their uniforms, the first two black, with brown and red labels, the third and smallest squad white, with transverse green sashes.[36]

The forms of objects that Joyce depicts in this image are symbols of solidity and rhythm. There is no atmosphere and the figures appear to form themselves in front of our eyes. They grow out of the surface of the picture.

Like Cézanne, whose impressionistic vision is not directed solely toward the observation of effects of light and color, Degas tends to search for the consequence of line and form in movement. This produces, according to Degas, an effective design: the curves of the figures are stressed by a heavy contour on the side from which the light comes in. The light that floods from one angle imparts unity to the image. In "Araby" Joyce represents a Degas-like image:

The light from the lamp opposite our door caught the white curve of her neck, lit up her hair that rested there and, falling, lit up the hand upon the railing. It fell over one side of her dress and caught the white border of a petticoat, just visible as she stood at ease.[37]

In conclusion, I would like to point out that the fusion of genres, the basis of the modern movement in art, led Joyce to experiment with impressionistic devices. With Poe and the impressionist painters he seeks the rarity of Beauty. He subscribes with Whistler and Poe to Bacon's doctrine that all Beauty must have in it some strangeness of proportion; strangeness is also an attribute of beauty according to Baudelaire who said "the beautiful is also bizarre."

In common with the impressionist painters, Joyce observes that there is no color peculiar to any object, but only more or less rapid vibrations of light upon its surface. A work of beauty, the ideal of all impressionists, elevates the soul (perhaps in conjunction with other faculties); it is distinguished by its indefiniteness—indefiniteness in its revelaton of image, of emotion and of concept. However, the impressionist movement in painting is only one of the major influences of modern painting on Joyce.

The later Joyce inclined to post-impressionism. In *Ulysses* the elaborate patterns of stylistic and structural devices are the result of Joyce's twin desires to imitate the impressions of reality, reproducing daily events directly, without comment—and to transform reality symbolically by showing the meaning that lies behind daily events.

CHAPTER SEVEN

James Joyce and De Chirico

With Poe and the other romantic authors the exterior world possesses no real autonomy and must depend upon the ego for animation and meaning. Thus every man becomes the creator of his own universe. Since the non-ego is a product of the imagination, the world becomes a vast poem which man is constantly inventing. The authors of this period substitute cosmic reconstruction for aesthetic construction. This is a major device of Poe, as Paul Valéry points out. In "Eureka" Poe "a bâti sur ces fondements mathématiques (la loi de la gravitation), un poème abstrait qui est un des rares exemplaires modernes d'une explication totale de la nature matérielle et spirituelle, une *cosmogonie*."[1]

Cosmic reconstruction is an aim common to the transcendentalists, such as the romantic, symbolist and surrealist writers and painters. Poe and Joyce achieve this cosmic reconstruction as we have seen in earlier chapters by breaking up the world of appearances into fragments, which are then rearranged according to a new order. With this new order the artists strive to reveal a superior reality. Thus literature and painting, for the romantic, symbolist, and surrealist writers and painters becomes an experience of vision. They unite not only nature and spirit, but, by confusing the senses with one another, they unite parts of this world.

The romantics have agreed that poetry is in some sense concerned with beauty. Poe asserts that it is concerned with nothing else and that its beauty is to be found through the search for supernal reality.

Within romanticism there is a liberation of the less conscious levels of the mind. The pure occupation of the romantics with their own selves and the consequent construction of worlds in which their own omnipotence may be exhibited stimulates the surrealists in their literature and painting to free expression of their states of consciousness. This tendency is significant, as Herbert Read points out:

> "Surrealism in general is the romantic principle in art."
> . . . With Baudelaire and Joyce and the surrealists complete understanding of the meaning of life consists in being able to perceive the relations between each element of our world and the various aspects of the transcendent entity that lies above and beyond. In certain privileged moments of mystic ecstasy it is possible to apprehend these subtle affinities.[2]

Poe, in "Eureka," describes the moment when the heart of man is confused with the heart of divinity. To Poe, Joyce, and their surrealist successors in painting, the beauty of a piece of prose or of a poem offers a means for spiritual perception or awareness. Through literature and painting we can perceive the beauty of the spiritual universe. The poet is a translator of this beauty of the universe which is the supreme unity. Poe, Joyce, and the surrealists express their belief in the world's unity. The region described in Baudelaire's "Invitation au Voyage" where "tout n'est qu'ordre et beauté" is that point where the human spirit participates in everything, where the one is apprehended as the multiple. This idea also Poe has expressed in "Eureka."

A complete reversal from the romantics' point of view takes place with the advent of impressionism and post-impressionism. Impressionism, on the one hand, has implied a dissolution of reality in the eyes of the artists, and post-impressionism, on the other hand, has produced deformation of reality. The latter engenders a complete disregard of actual proportions and forms. Cézanne then is among the first modern painters who deliberately refuses to copy nature and sets out to reshape and reorganize all its elements according to the rhythm of his own sensibility. The all important artistic inspiration is no longer the forms and aspects of nature, but the soul of the artist himself.

As we know, Poe bases his aesthetics on the bipartite soul; this Poe illustrates with the creative and resolvent faculties of his detectives, with the split between rational and irrational faculties of man. Joyce, in depicting Stephen's early childhood, exploits rational images and actions to disguise irrational emotional content as early as in "Dubliners." Joyce relates his stories in a series of rational, realistic, recognizable images imbedded in an almost but not quite nightmarish texture. This impression the reader gathers with the opening pages of "A Portrait of the Artist," when Stephen finds himself on the wide playgrounds. In this image the tangibility of texture and the solidity of forms contrast with the reality beyond the appearances. Like Giorgio de Chirico in "Departure of a Poet," in "Gare Montparnasse," and in "The Anguish of Departure," Joyce suggests a wistful, nostalgic atmosphere of a world in which the impossible mingles with the possible and in which time and space are other than those of the real world:

> The wide playgrounds were swarming with boys. All were shouting and the prefects urged them on with strong cries. The evening air was pale and chilly and after every charge and thud of the footballers the greasy leather orb flew like a heavy bird through the grey light. He kept on the fringe of his line, out of sight of his prefect, out of the reach of the rude feet, feigning to run now and then. He felt his body small and weak amid the throng of players and his eyes were weak and watery.[3]

In Poe's, Joyce's and de Chirico's work the strict formal structures communicate in their arrangement an ideal reality that is of metaphysical significance. This metaphysical reality is represented sometimes with geometrical planes, by a number of apparently disconnected symbols in the world of appearance: a color, an odor, an emotion, an event, a musical aria may all possess the same symbolical significance and may therefore be interchanged without disturbing the fundamental harmony that lies at the heart of things. The imagination has to make coherent an infinite variety of impressions, ideas, and forms. Thereby Poe, de Chirico, and Joyce go so deeply into psychoanalytic exploration that they pass beyond the personal reminiscence into the universal. This de Chirico realizes with the representation of human beings in mathematical forms and planes, translating these geometrical human beings as portentous symbols of a higher reality. De Chirico illustrates these types of human beings with planes in paintings such as "The Mathematicians," "The Apparition," and "The Return." The moment when Stephen arrives at the center of himself and thus at the center of human destiny, as the end paragraph of "A Portrait of the Artist" suggests, or when Stephen participates in the consciousness of the world and establishes there a point of contact between himself and the world, then Stephen is a surrealist who represents his vision in geometrical planes in the way de Chirico has conceived it.

> He [Stephen] closed his eyes in the languor of sleep. His eyelids trembled as if they felt the vast cyclic movement of the earth and her watchers, trembled as if they felt the strange light of some new world. His soul was swooning into some new world, fantastic, dim, uncertain as under sea, traversed by cloudy shapes and beings. A world, a glimmer, or a flower? Glimmering and trembling, trembling and unfolding, a breaking light, an opening flower. . . . Oh, the grey dull day! It seemed a limbo of painless patient consciousness through which souls of mathematicians might wander, projecting long slender fabrics from plane to plane of ever rarer and paler twilight, radiating swift eddies to the last verges of a universe ever faster, farther, and more impalpable.[4]

Poe's interest, as we have seen in previous chapters, is concentrated on the power of the imagination. In "Eureka," Poe expresses the belief that the imagination is not simply that faculty of the poet which creates and combines images, not merely fancy, as Coleridge would have said, but that it is a creative power, a means by which beauty can be embodied in a poem.

Poe's lesson on the autonomy of the imagination is to become a principal article of surrealist faith. The imagination for Poe, Joyce, and the surrealist painters is the faculty able to call upon the subconscious forces that foreshadow another reality. Poe's protagonist Usher has "to inter his sister's body in an underground vault, thus fulfilling the desire of which his painting was the prophetic, and almost surrealistic, representation."[5]

Poe and de Chirico have recognized that our subconscious minds influence our thought when liberated by sleep. De Chirico's paintings represent the metaphysical universe of the city; it is a world of dreams in which from the extreme clearness of details arises a new reality.

> Quasi sempre si tratta di personaggi di città imaginarie, che sembrano sorti davanti all'artista durante il sogno, nei quali gli elementi fantastici si intrecciano con i ricordi delle cose vedute e vissute e la realtà è trasfigurata, "resa strana."[6]

De Chirico, Poe, and Joyce at times turn all their perceptive faculties inwards, to the realm of their subjective fancies, daydreams, and preconscious images. The way they achieve their associations of past and present foreshadows the surrealists. They attempt to escape from everyday reality into the realm of memory of the subconscious. Poe, de Chirico, and Joyce *"find"* profound experiences and profound pictures which they try to bring to light through their writing. They believe that they are able to penetrate the realm of the unconscious as de Chirico illustrates in "The Portrait of Apollinaire" with the explanation: "Ce que j'écoute ne vaut rien; il n'y que ce que mes yeux voient ouverts ou plus encore fermés."[7] These writers attempt with de Chirico to reach a level at which man is an essential part of the universe. They move steadily in the direction of an art of dreamed sensation. Obviously, Poe, de Chirico, and Joyce aim at a lucid quality that Breton describes as the integrity of a dream. With them as for "the surrealists, reality is only to be found in the images and symbols of an inner world; it is to be found therefore in art."[8]

In the second *Manifesto* Breton summarizes the attempt of the surrealists to unify interior and exterior reality. This final unification, Breton emphasizes, is the supreme aim of surrealism, since these two forms of reality, interior and exterior, are in contradiction to one another in the present form of society.

Throughout their work, de Chirico and Joyce stress the existence of two realities, the exterior and the interior. De Chirico symbolically represents these two realities in "The Slumber," stressing a movement out of the city with the images of a leaving train and a white sailing vessel at the moment of departure. There is a chimney, the smoke of which transcends a high wall. In contrast to these images of a motion out of the city, de Chirico represents in the center of the painting a man asleep, symbolizing the concentration on himself and the self-sufficient isolation of a human being. In Joyce's "Dubliners" there is a steady movement out of and into the city, a centrifugal and centripetal motion. The first chapter of "A Portrait of the Artist" leads the reader symbolically twenty miles outside of the city to Clongowes, and the later chapters lead back again to the city, which steadily becomes an image of Stephen's psyche. In *Ulysses* the contrast of these two realities, outer and inner, is represented in the image of outward and inward bound trams.

In Joyce's work the description of Dublin transforms itself from a memory into a dream image. In "A Portrait of the Artist" scene dissolves into scene, action dissolves into action, in a gradually descending curve. Scenes, action, people, images are caught up in the rhythmic repetition of dream distortions, where even the sentence-to-sentence movement is consonant with the basic form, expressing Stephen's inability to concretize his position:

> He peered out for an instant over the coverlet and saw the yellow curtains round and before his bed that shut him off on all sides. . . . A figure came up the staircase from the hall. . . . Going home for the holidays! That would be lovely: the fellows had told him. Getting up on the cars in the early wintry morning outside the door of the castle. The cars were rolling on the gravel. Cheers for the rector! . . . Cheer after cheer after cheer. . . . The

peasant women stood at the half doors, the men stood here and there. The lovely smell there was in the wintry air: the smell of Clane: rain and wintry air and turf smouldering and corduroy. The train was full of fellows: a long chocolate train with cream facings. . . . They were men in dark blue and silver; they had silvery whistles and their keys made a quick music: click, click: click, click. And the train raced on over the flat lands and past the Hill of Allen. . . . There were lanterns in the hall of his father's house and ropes of green branches. . . . There was a noise of curtainrings. . . . He got up and sat on the side of his bed. He was weak. He tried to pull on his stocking. It had a horrid rough feel. The sunlight was queer and cold.[9]

Joyce embodies in the larger part of his work repetitions of a scene, a series of images, a single image or a situation in "other words" or "other forms." De Chirico creates similar effects with the repeated representations of leaving trains and vessels, high towers and huge walls, with large open spaces and lurking archways, images that Joyce frequently evokes, in ever new geometrical arrangements.

The typical de Chirico city reappears in *Ulysses*. "Metaphysical disquietude" overcomes Stephen whenever he is aware of his strange and large environment. When Stephen walks along the strand the image of a strange land with threatening faces, with shadows of monuments and dark apertures, is disclosed to him. As in de Chirico's later paintings such as in "The Sailors' Barracks" there are no bright tones, yet more recessive planes of shadow and sudden pools of darkness:

Walk along a strand, strange land, come to a city gate, sentry there, old ranker too, old Tweedy's big moustaches leaning on a long kind of spear. Wander through awned streets. Turbaned faces going by. Dark caves of carpet shops, big man, Turko the terrible, seated cross-legged smoking a coiled pipe. Cries of sellers in the streets. Drink water scented with fennel, sherbet. Wander along all day. Might meet a robber or two. Well, meet him. Getting on to sundown. The shadows of the mosques along the pillars: priests with a scroll rolled up. A shiver of the trees, signal, the evening wind. I pass on. Fading gold sky. A mother watches from her doorway. She calls her children home in their dark language. High wall: beyond strings twanged. Night sky moon, violet, colour of Molly's new garters. Strings. Listen. A girl playing one of these instruments what do you call them: dulcimers. I pass.[10]

Thus Joyce creates, as does de Chirico, dream images with fantastic juxtapositions that are full of mysterious meaning. Both Joyce and de Chirico charge the cold and pure atmosphere with mystery or an undercurrent of meaning. The largeness of space suggests something unnatural. De Chirico and Joyce stress the effect of these dream-like scenes by contrasting the largeness of space with objects that seem to be insignificant. Thus Joyce in "The Sisters" depicts an unassuming shop in a little house and contrasts it with its location on Great Britain Street. The unnatural elements Joyce frequently interweaves in his early work: "The drapery consisted mainly of children's booties and umbrellas; and on ordinary days a notice used to hang in the window, saying *Umbrellas Re-covered*."[11] Another instance is in the scene when Stephen tries to decipher the legend on a Norwegian vessel. There predominates a mysterious, unnatural atmosphere. Thus Stephen's environment and his schoolmates appear under the arbitrariness of a more real reality. The mysterious, dream-like scenes, the large and shadowy environment, the new school of modern painters would have called the *réalité absolue* or the surreality. In these dream-like scenes there are yawning, cavernous apertures, openings, doors, arches and windows that are closely related to the figures. These induce foreboding of cosmic mystery, as the "lighted square of window"[12] suggests in the opening passage of "The Sisters." With the paintings of de Chirico, such as "The Joy of Return" or "The Departure of the Poet," these apertures lead the protagonists into another world. De Chirico and Joyce depict protagonists who live under the impression that everything gazes at them. De Chirico says:

"Everything has two aspects: the current aspect which we see
. . . and the ghostly and metaphysical aspect, which only rare
individuals may see in moments of clairvoyance and metaphysical
abstraction."[13]

As discussed in an earlier chapter, the relationship of objects
in space is significant to Poe and Joyce. With these relationships
between objects both authors convey, in a way as de Chirico
conceives it in "The Melancholy of Departure," the feeling of
threat, disquietude, and anxiety. Stephen's environment has an
elegiac beauty and vast dignity, filled with profound silences.
With these silences Joyce expresses as de Chirico does, a kind of
surreality. Stephen explains himself: "By his monstrous way of
life he seemed to have put himself beyond the limits of reality.[14]
De Chirico and Joyce attempt that which has been achieved by
the surrealists, to discover behind the enigmatic silence and
aloofness of the natural world its latent meaning. This latent
meaning of a silent, mysterious atmosphere Joyce suggests in
"A Portrait of the Artist." Behind the disquieting stillness Joyce
creates, as does de Chirico, a meaningful drama. This drama
progresses with the conjunction of inanimate objects.

Both artists fix in their pictures something remote, nostalgic
and haunting. At the same time they convey with the aloofness
of silence a feeling of agonized suspense, an expectation of some
impending catastrophe of, presumably, a supernatural order.
Thus in "Anguish of Departure" de Chirico creates an atmosphere of strangeness and nostalgia by the vast expanse of space,
the long shadows and the train departing in the distance. This
atmosphere of utter silence is conveyed to the reader through
architecture, figures, objects, and statuary, that appear to be
utterly detached from a near and present-day reality. Thus silence
is closely associated with the concept of space. This is what
Joyce represents in *Ulysses*, with the reconciliation of the op-
posites, sounds and silence:

> The voices blend and fuse in clouded silence: silence
> that is the infinite of space: and swiftly, silently the soul
> is wafted over regions of cycles of cycles of generations
> that have lived.[15]

In de Chirico's and Joyce's work there is within the vibrating silence a waiting for a cry or a whistle. The effect is intensified by both artists, with the impression that behind their geometrical precisions of a quadrangle there is another world inaccessible to visible perceptions. In *Ulysses* this effect is further produced by something concealed behind the mask of a gardener and the immobility of his countenance:

> Shouts from the open window startling evening in the quadrangle. A deaf gardener, aproned, masked with Matthew Arnold's face, pushes his mower on the sombre lawn watching narrowly the dancing motes of grass-halms. . . . Let him stay, Stephen said. There's nothing wrong with him except at night.[16]

Although this image is depicted with apparent realism, the immobility of the gardner's features and his deafness suggest a world of the gardener's own, full of mysterious portents that are his life force. The cry or whistle in a vibrating silence brings the protagonists of Joyce and de Chirico in connection with another world that is inaccessible to their limited capacity of visual perception under normal conditions: Stephen identifies this kind of shout with a goal that is the manifestation of God to him:

> From the playfield the boys raised a shout. A whirring whistle: goal. What if that nightmare gave you a back kick?
> —The ways of the Creator are not our ways, Mr. Deasy said. All history moves towards one great goal, the manifestation of God.
> Stephen jerked his thumb towards the window, saying:
> —That is God.
> Hooray! Ay! Whrrwhee!
> —What? Mr. Deasy asked.
> A shout in the street, Stephen answered, shrugging his shoulders.[17]

Thus for Joyce, as for de Chirico, there seems to be on the other side of visual perception a world full of mysterious portents. These are most expressive in de Chirico's oppressively deserted

Italian towns, such as in "The Anxious Journey." The arcades of de Chirico's palaces, look like hugely gaping eyes whose depths reveal nothing but a void impossible to plumb. Similarly, in Joyce's work, although all events seem natural enough, everything is ominous in this queer, *unheimlichen* vision of the world; this Stephen experiences as early as "The Sisters":

> The reading of the card persuaded me that he [the priest] was dead and I was disturbed to find myself at check. Had he not been dead I would have gone into the little dark room behind the shop to find him sitting in his arm-chair by the fire, nearly smothered in his great-coat. Perhaps my aunt would have given me a packet of High Toast for him and this present would have roused him from his stupefied doze. It was always I who emptied the packet into his black snuff-box for his hands trembled too much to allow him to do this without spilling half the snuff about the floor.[18]

As this image shows, Joyce, instead of creating the formal relationships of objects, stresses those of moods and feelings as de Chirico in his paintings.

Both de Chirico and Joyce were influenced by Nietzsche during their stay in Munich. De Chirico accepts from Nietzsche an outstanding innovation, as he writes in his autobiography:

> This innovation is a strange and profound poetry, infinitely mysterious and solitary, based on *Stimmung* (which might be translated as atmosphere), based I say, on the *Stimmung* of an autumn afternoon, when the weather is clear and the shadows are longer than in summer, for the sun is beginning to be lower.[19]

De Chirico's paintings convey the mood of an ominous, impending event. The predominant mood is that of emptiness and the void. A metaphysical nihilism is the substance of de Chirico's work, as the "Enigma of a Day" suggests. This emptiness of de Chirico's paintings is at the same time the dominant theme of Poe, Mallarmé, Joyce, and the surrealist painters. Stephen, aware of this emptiness has the secret desire to leave the known and habitual life in order to explore the unknown and the strange. With each successive story or chapter, Stephen explores deeper and deeper the world of the unconscious. Stephen descends into what Pascal calls the "abyss," namely, the depth of his subconscious being. In Joyce's work, especially in "A Portrait of the Artist," all the elaborate images which Stephen unfolds, serve as a kind of springboard from which he leaps into the void. This Stephen experiences when he imagines himself an actor on a stage, and suddenly he becomes aware of the emptiness of the present. Reality falls asunder:

> A few moments after he found himself on the stage amid the garish gas and the dim scenery, acting before the innumerable faces of the void. . . . When the curtain fell on the last scene he heard the void filled with applause and . . . saw the simple body before which he had acted magically deformed, the void of faces breaking at all points and falling asunder into busy groups.[20]

In this emptiness, in this experience of the void, Joyce, like Rimbaud who knows that "Je est un autre," watches in "A Portrait of the Artist" the birth of his own thought and experiences of early childhood, as if these were rising up from the depths of a being different from his own being. Like Rimbaud, Stephen in the above-quoted scene feels to be the observer of the birth of his own personality; "J'assiste [Rimbaud] à l'éclosion de ma pensée: je la regarde, je l'écoute." Stephen, as an artist in *Ulysses*, makes this self-revelation the very essence of his aesthetic principle. He abstracts from an image of everyday reality all the essential features; nothing but the void remains:

> . . . all those elements which he deemed common and insignificant fell out of the scene. There remained no trace of the tram itself nor of the trammen nor of the horses: nor did he and she appear vividly.[21]

Joyce's poetic experience compares with that of Poe and de Chirico in his conception that his will has the power to make external reality into anything it wishes and to shape it into anything the imagination decrees. Thus they create an illusory atmosphere. Both de Chirico and Joyce create this illusory atmosphere with perspectives by means of ever-receding horizons. The arbitrary perspective of buildings and tramlines foretells the extension of space, as de Chirico suggests it in "Gare Montparnasse" or in "Still Life: Turin 1913." These perspectives reach out into infinity and seem to have architectural significance of the same kind as any other architectural forms. A spatial magic arises from this use of perspective. The concept of space becomes in de Chirico's as in Joyce's work an all-pervading factor. Thus in "A Portrait of the Artist" the flying lines of tables cut the immobility of space:

> . . . the higher line fellows began to come along the matting in the middle of the refectory. . . . And then the lower line tables and the tables of the third line.[22]

An illusory perspective is created in *Ulysses* with the image of straight lines of trams, in centrifugal and centripetal direction, leading from Bloom's position into the infinite and then returning to Bloom:

> Retreating, at the terminus of the Great Northern Railway, Amiens street, with constant uniform acceleration, along parallel lines meeting at infinity, if produced: along parallel lines reproduced from infinity, with constant uniform retardation at the terminus of the Great Northern Railway, Amiens street returning.[23]

Another way of creating illusory perspective de Chirico and Joyce represent by the evocation of sound effects at a certain distance: thus de Chirico defines the horizon by a wall behind which rises the noise of a disappearing train in "The Anguish of Departure," "Gare Montparnasse," "Departure of a Poet," as does Joyce in "Eveline" where from beside the quay wall a "mournful whistle" blows into the mist. With the evocation of vastness and distance through the suggestion of distant sounds Joyce creates perspective which symbolizes the infinite.

> The fellows seemed to him to have grown smaller: that was because a sprinter had knocked him down the day before, the fellow out of second of grammar. He had been thrown by the fellow's machine lightly on the cinderpath and his spectacles had been broken in three pieces and some of the grit of the cinders had gone into his mouth.
>
> That was why the fellows seemed to him smaller and farther away and the goalposts so thin and far and the soft grey sky so high up. But there was no play on the football grounds for cricket was coming: and some said that Barnes would be prof and some said it would be Flowers. And all over the playgrounds they were playing rounders and bowling twisters and lobs. And from here and from there came the sounds of the cricket bats through the soft grey air. They said: pick, pack, pock, puck: little drops of water in a fountain slowly falling in the brimming bowl.[24]

Joyce and de Chirico evoke a world of utter silence in which the bright arcades with long architectural recessions repeat themselves *ad infinitum*. The perspective of lines that lead nowhere and the labyrinth of arches through which Joyce's and de Chirico's protagonists wander convey a feeling of ultimate anxiety and terror. An atmosphere of emptiness and of the void prevails. Thus de Chirico's "Anxious Journey" seems to be closely related with Stephen's nightmarish journey through tunnels; both de Chirico and Joyce frequently evoke, as these images show, a wall for indicating a distant horizon. The wall stimulates the spectator to explore the reality behind the wall:

> First came the vacation and then the next term and then vacation again and then again another term and then again vacation. It was like a train going in and out of tunnels and that was like the noise of the boys eating in

the refectory when you opened and closed the flaps of
the ears. Term, vacation; tunnel, out; noise, stop. How
far away it was! . . . The bell rang for night prayers and
he filed out of the study hall after the others and down
the staircase and along the corridors to the chapel. . . .
The sea was cold day and night: but it was cold and
dark under the seawall beside his father's house.[25]

Thus, both de Chirico and Joyce project their images or pictures
on the basis of a far-reaching spatial environment. They create
the illusion of endless distance as de Chirico's "Melancholy of
Departure" or the image of Joyce, quoted above, indicate. They
use the device of perspective. A colonnade or a tunnel with
rapidly diminishing arches or goalposts intensifies the illusion of
limitless space.

Joyce stresses with de Chirico that everything has two aspects,
the current and the metaphysical aspect. The city is the scene of
almost all their works. They both depict broken columns and
fragments of statuary; there are indifferent monuments in large
spaces full of tragic portents behind which is hidden a metaphysical reality:

He [Stephen] turned into Cumberland street and, going
on some paces, halted in the lee of the station wall. No-
one. Meade's timberyard. Piled balks. Ruins and tene-
ments. With careful tread he passed over a hopscotch
court with its forgotten pickeystone. Not a sinner. Near
the timberyard a squatted child at marbles, alone, shoot-
ing the taw with a cunnythumb. A wise tabby, a blink-
ing sphinx, watched from her warm sill. Pity to disturb
them. Mohammed cut a piece out of his mantle not to
wake her. Open it[26]

The image of the city offers infinite escapes by way of colon-
nades, straight lines, and memory evocations of birds in flight.
Over their city hovers a pathetic melancholy. There seems to be
a hidden reality in the flight of birds over the city, as de Chirico
suggests in "The Enigma of a Day" and Joyce in "A Portrait of

the Artist." Although man has observed these strange birds for ages, only the writer has the clairvoyance to perceive their symbolic meanings:

> And for ages men had gazed upward as he was gazing at birds in flight. The colonnade above him made him think vaguely of an ancient temple and the ashplant on which he leaned wearily of the curved stick of an augur. A sense of fear of the unknown moved in the heart of his weariness, a fear of symbols and portents, of the hawklike man whose name he bore soaring out of his captivity on osierwoven wings, of Thoth, the god of writers, writing with a reed upon a tablet and bearing on his narrow ibis head the cusped moon.[27]

In this image Joyce achieves, as de Chirico does, an association of past and present. Time seems to be immobilized, since past and future are present at once.

They both agree with the surrealists in their belief that the emotions or feelings may come from every possible source: a window, a poster or a word. They show that the universe opens itself to our curiosity by an unforeseen combination of actual and fantastic things. Thereby they follow closely what Poe has accomplished: they assert with Poe that the poet does not actually create beauty in the literal sense of creation; he merely combines what already exists in nature and lifts the combination into beauty by the addition of elements of the mystic or the ideal. Upon this position Poe draws in his "Poetic Principle." Poe considers the poem, as repeatedly stated, to be that class of composition in which there lies beneath the transparent upper current of meaning an undercurrent or suggestive one. With this objective in mind, de Chirico and Joyce represent objects that are well known to us in daily life, in strict juxtaposition. Thereby they show how the universe opens itself to our curiosity, by an unforeseen combination of actual and fantastic things, of the "elements of surprise" as Apollinaire would have called them. Joyce's and de Chirico's objects, vegetables, fruits or dry biscuits are all represented with absolute indifference. They are so impersonal that they lose all of their natural meaning. The apparent chance disposition of certain objects may awaken responses which the individual is at a loss to explain. The elements of surprise form an enigma of revelation.

A sound and a line of thought suddenly merge by chance to produce an imagined sound which itself introduces appropriate visual imagery. Bloom states this type of modality of the audible in *Ulysses*:

> What was I saying Barrels? Gallons. About a million barrels all the same.
> An incoming train clanked heavily above his head, coach after coach. Barrels bumped in his head: dull porter slopped and churned inside. The bungholes sprang open and a huge dull flood leaked, flowing together, winding through mudflats all over the level land, a lazy pooling swirl of liquor bearing along wide-leaved flowers of its froth.[28]

De Chirico and Joyce introduce us into a magic and strange world. It has been depicted in a similar way by writers such as Poe, and Rimbaud, by painters such as Picasso. The masterpieces of these authors show certain childlike qualities, since, as the critic Münsterberg says,

> to become really immortal, a work of art must escape all human limits, logic and common sense will only interfere. But once the barriers are broken it will enter the regions of childhood vision and dream.[29]

Thus the high walls, the immobility of the observers in Joyce's "An Encounter" affirm a certain stability of their dreams and desires that seem to be closely related to those of de Chirico's protagonists. Thus in the image that follows there is a chance disposition of currant buns, a metal piping, and a big white sailing vessel that evoke in the reader responses similar to those of de Chirico's paintings such as the chance objects in the "Sailors' Barracks."

We [Stephen and Mahony] came near the river. We spent a long time walking about the noisy streets flanked by high stone walls, watching the working of cranes and engines and often being shouted at for our immobility by the drivers of groaning carts. It was noon when we reached the quays and, as all the labourers seemed to be eating their lunches, we bought two big currant buns and sat down to eat them on some metal piping beside the river. We pleased ourselves with the spectacle of Dublin's commerce—the barges signalled from far away by their curls of woolly smoke, the brown fishing fleet beyond Ringsend, the big white sailingvessel which was being discharged on the opposite quay.[30]

This image shows that for Stephen sensations, horizons, and objects in a certain chance disposition exist in an endless variety and cinematographic succession; they affirm the permanence of his human being.

Joyce's and de Chirico's metaphysical universe is closely related to the universe of dreams, where the precision of details results in a new reality, secret and unpredictable. The world in which they live seems to them large and monumental. They reveal to us the nostalgia of the infinite behind the geometrical precision of a square, as de Chirico's "Gare Montparnasse" suggests. This kind of nostalgia of the infinite Stephen evokes when he crosses a quadrangle with his friend Cranly, shouts penetrate the soft still air from far away. Stephen is then alone in front of a polished hotel, waiting:

Stephen walked on alone and out into the quiet of Kildare Street opposite Maple's hotel he stood to wait, patient again. The name of the hotel, a colourless polished wood, and its colourless front stung him like a glance of polite disdain.[31]

It seems that Joyce's and de Chirico's protagonists frequently stop and wait in anxiety for a coming event.

Parallel with this anxious suspense of waiting in the works of both, of de Chirico and Joyce, there is a nostalgia of railway stations, of arrivals and departures. The theme of belatedness pervades their representations. Thus in de Chirico's paintings, "The Transformed Dream," "The Square," "The Uncertainty of the Poet," "The Chimney," the spectator is made to feel that he has just missed a train. A similar characteristic the critic Julian B. Kaye observes in Joyce's work:

> In "The Sisters" we see the boy narrator with the dead father Flynn and his two aged and decrepit sisters. He seems bound to them and to the dead and dying past which they represent. In "Araby" he arrives at a bazaar —the object of another enthusiastic expedition—just before closing time on the last day.[32]

In conclusion, all these effects that de Chirico and Joyce convey, represent an attempt to discover the world as it is on the other side of visual perception. A poetic disquietude and anxiety predominates their work. De Chirico and Joyce share in the desire of Poe to release the reality which is concealed behind the screen of commonplace. In contradistinction from the surrealists, de Chirico, Joyce and Poe do not attempt a liberation of the subconscious by an extreme separation of this level of experience from the levels of intellect and reason. In common with the surrealists, however, they create dream-like, fantastic images which are effectively combined with a formally beautiful composition. Poe, de Chirico, and Joyce have a metaphysical sensibility to combine things not according to their logical relationships, but according to their essence and spiritual analogies revealed to the imagination. The power of the imagination is a central point of Poe's, de Chirico's, Joyce's and Breton's aesthetics. Breton considers Edgar Allan Poe the main source of his conception of the imagination, when he says:

> L'imagination pure, dit Poe, choisit soit dans le Beau, soit dans le Laid, les seuls éléments qui n'ayant jamais été associés encore conviennent le plus avantageusement à ses combinaisons. Le composé ainsi obtenu revêt toujours un caractère de beauté ou de sublimité propor-

tionnel aux qualités respectives des parties mises en présence, lesquelles doivent être considérées elles-mêmes comme résultant de combinaisons antérieurement réalisées. Or, par une singulière analogie entre les phénomènes chimiques naturels et ceux de la chimie de l'intelligence, il arrive souvent que la réunion des deux éléments donne naissance à un produit nouveau qui ne rappelle plus rien des qualités de tel ou tel composant, ni même d'aucun d'eux.[33]

Their attempt may be brought to a common denominator: to make with the power of the imagination materials become ideas. This Joyce realized in *Finnegans Wake*.

Epilogue

The purpose of this study has been to approach an understanding of Joyce's imagery by a comparison with that of Poe, some French symbolists, and some modern painters. With Joyce's imagery a very characteristic and certainly the most original development of the aesthetic of imagery has been made in the twentieth century.

The imagery of the discussed artists reveals a world of their intuitions and illusions. The writing and painting of the discussed artists is full of allusions and suggestions, since they all have confidence in the eternal correspondences between the visible and the invisible universe, which Poe and the French symbolists taught. By means of the suggestive power of words and images they reveal the essential kinship of all things and souls in an all-pervasive mind, in the profound unity of the world that they perceive. "Peindre non la chose, mais l'effet qu'elle produit" summarizes their common attempt. Stephen's change from the direct and immediate sensations of childhood and adolescence to that of the more structured, organized sensations of an adult parallel the change of the impressionist painters who became dissatisfied with the formlessness and superficial quality of the recording of immediately perceived sensations and who turned to the more ordered structure of the post-impressionists. With Poe and the surrealists, Joyce tries to get beneath the surface of things, to get the undercurrent of meaning. To go beyond reality and to extend the range of vision is an ideal of modern art. A sense of the deep life of the spirit, a certain intuition of mystery and of a reality transcending the phenomenal world, a new will to grasp the essence of things, to free it from didacticism and sentimentalism, to suggest a mysterious reality hidden behind the world of perception starts with Poe.

Poe, Joyce, and the discussed modern painters auscult their own selves before turning to the universe. They attempt to make their literature and painting an instrument of knowledge. They dream to transcend man. They have a sense of the deep life of the spirit, a certain intuition of mystery and of a reality transcending the phenomenal world. With Poe, Joyce, and the surrealists there is a progressive deepening spiritualization of their visions. Thereby they express their belief that beyond the limits of this world lies an invisible, supernatural universe.

Thus, for Poe, Joyce, and these modern painters the complete understanding of the meaning of life consists in being able to perceive the relations between each element of our world and the various aspects of the transcendent entity that lies above and beyond. The theories and imagery of Poe stand as a signpost at the very threshold of the present era.

Notes

Chapter One

1. James Joyce, *The Critical Writings of James Joyce*, ed. Ellsworth Mason and Richard Ellmann (New York: The Viking Press, 1959), p. 80.

2. James Joyce, *The Portable James Joyce* (New York: The Viking Press, 1958), p. 49.

3. *Ibid.*, p. 242.

4. *Ibid.*, p. 260.

5. *Ibid.*, p. 191, and James Joyce, *Ulysses* (New York: The Modern Library, 1946), p. 654.

6. James Joyce, *Finnegans Wake* (London: Faber & Faber, 1939), p. 3.

7. *The Portable James Joyce*, p. 249.

8. *Ibid.*, p. 39, and James Joyce, *Stephen Hero* (New York: New Directions, 1955), p. 70.

9. *Finnegans Wake*, p. 420.

10. *Ibid.*, p. 489.

11. *Ulysses*, p. 137.

12. *Finnegans Wake*, p. 534.

13. *Ibid.*, p. 326.

14. *Ibid.*, pp. 20-22.

15. *Ibid.*, p. 588.

16. Harro Heinz Kühnelt, *Die Bedeutung von Edgar Allan Poe in der englischen Literatur* (Universität Innsbruck: Innsbruck, 1949).

17. *Ibid.*, p. 301.

18. Frank Budgen, "Further Recollections of James Joyce," *Partisan Review*, XXIII (Fall, 1956), 530-44.

19. Edward Shanks, *Edgar Allan Poe* (New York: The Macmillan Company, 1937), p. 195.

20. Herbert Gorman, *James Joyce* (New York: Rinehart and Company, Inc., 1948), p. 178.

21. Harro Heinz Kühnelt, "T. S. Eliot als Poe-Kritiker," *Die Neueren Sprachen*, Heft 3 (1956), p. 107.

22. By an epiphany he meant a sudden spiritual manifestation, whether in the vulgarity of speech or of gesture or in a memorable phase of the mind itself. He [Stephen] believed that it was for the

man of letters to record these epiphanies with extreme care, seeing that they themselves are the most delicate and evanescent of moments. *Stephen Hero*, p. 211. See also: Irene Hendry, "Joyce's Epiphanies," *James Joyce: Two Decades of Criticism*, ed. Seon Givens (New York: The Vanguard Press, 1948), pp. 27-46.

23. Edgar Allan Poe, "The Poetic Principle," *The Complete Works of Edgar Allan Poe*, ed. James A. Harrison (17 vols.; New York: Society of English and French Literature, 1902), XIV, 274-75.

24. Gorman, p. 220.

25. Ezra Pound, "Letter to Harriet Monroe, January 31, 1915," *The Letters of Ezra Pound, 1907-1941*, ed. D. D. Paige (New York: Harcourt, Brace and Co., 1950), p. 50.

26. Ezra Pound, *Literary Essays* (Norfolk, Conn.: New Directions, n.d.), p. 218.

27. David Hayman, *James Joyce et Mallarmé* (2 vols.; Paris: Lettres Modernes, 1956) I, 27-32.

28. Max Wildi, "Arthur Symons als Kritiker der Literatur," *Anglistische Forschungen*, Heft 67 (Dissertation, Heidelberg, 1929), p. 33.

29. Hayman, I, 32.

30. Joris-Karl Huysmans, *À Rebours*, Bibliothèque Charpentier (Paris: Facquelle Editeurs, n.d.).

31. Arthur Symons, "Joris-Karl Huysmans," *The Symbolist Movement in Literature* (New York: E. P. Dutton and Co., 1919), p. 249.

32. Translated from Huysmans, *À Rebours* in *ibid.*, p. 257.

33. Huysmans, p. 255.

34. Symons, p. 247.

35. Huysmans, p. 183.

36. Symons, p. 247.

37. Huysmans, pp. 222-23.

38. Symons, p. 196.

39. Paul Verlaine, *Les Poètes Maudits* (Paris: Léon Vannier, 1884).

40. Hayman, I, 26.

41. Symons, pp. 195-96.

42. Poe, *The Complete Works of Edgar Allan Poe*, XIV, 208.

43. Camille Mauclair, *Le Genie d'Edgar Poe* (Paris: Albin Michel, 1926), p. 92.

44. Symons, p. 146.

45. William York Tindall, *James Joyce: His Way of Interpreting the Modern World* (New York: Charles Scribner's Sons, 1950), p. 110.

46. *The Complete Works of Edgar Allan Poe*, XIV, 208.

47. Arthur Symons, *Figures of Several Centuries* (London: Constable and Co., Ltd., 1916), pp. 117-18.

48. *The Critical Writings of James Joyce*, p. 80.

49. *Oeuvres Complètes de Paul Verlaine* (Paris: Albert Messein, éditeur, 1926), IV, 46. See also Camille Mauclair, *Le Génie d'Edgar Poe* (Paris: Albin Michel, 1926), p. 278.

50. Symons, *Symbolist Movement in Literature*, p. 183.

51. Hayman, I, 32.

52. *Ibid.*, I, 38.

53. William York Tindall, *The Literary Symbol* (New York: Columbia University Press, 1955), p. 37.

54. *The Portable James Joyce*, p. 11.

55. Letter to Dujardin by André Gide, July 4, 1930, in Édouard Dujardin, *Le Monologue Intérieur*, ed. Albert Massein (Paris, 1931), p. 66.

56. *Ibid.*, p. 66.

57. Francis Thompson, *Literary Criticisms*, Newly Discovered and Collected by Rev. Terence L. Connolly (New York: E. P. Dutton and Co., Inc., 1948), p. 365.

58. Edmund Wilson, *Axel's Castle* (New York & London: Charles Scribner's Sons, 1939), pp. 1, 17.

59. Enid Starkie, *From Gautier to Eliot* (London: Hutchinson, 1960), p. 187.

Chapter Two

1. Edgar Allan Poe, *The Complete Tales and Poems of Edgar Allan Poe* (New York: The Modern Library, 1938), p. 645.

2. Carl G. Jung, *Die Wirklichkeit der Seele* (Rascher Verlag: Zürich, 1939), p. 146.

3. *The Portable James Joyce*, pp. 421-22.

4. *The Complete Tales and Poems of Edgar Allan Poe*, p. 383.

5. *Ibid.*, p. 137.

6. *Ulysses*, p. 111.

7. *The Complete Tales and Poems of Edgar Allan Poe*, p. 233.

8. *Ibid.*, pp. 57-58.

9. *Ibid.*, p. 221.

10. *The Portable James Joyce*, p. 433.

11. *The Complete Tales and Poems of Edgar Allan Poe*, p. 249.

12. *The Portable James Joyce*, p. 74.

13. *Ibid.*, p. 354.

14. *Ibid.*, p. 370.

15. *The Complete Tales and Poems of Edgar Allan Poe*, p. 701.

16. *The Portable James Joyce*, p. 308.

17. *Stephen Hero*, p. 186.

18. *The Portable James Joyce*, p. 407.

19. *Ulysses*, p. 682.

20. *The Complete Tales and Poems of Edgar Allan Poe*, p. 449.
21. *The Portable James Joyce*, p. 241-42.
22. *The Complete Works of Edgar Allan Poe*, XVI, 2.
23. *The Complete Tales and Poems of Edgar Allan Poe*, p. 286.
24. *The Literary Symbol*, p. 66.
25. *The Portable James Joyce*, p. 255.
26. *Ibid.*
27. *Ibid.*, p. 427.
28. *The Complete Tales and Poems of Edgar Allan Poe*, p. 656.
29. *The Complete Works of Edgar Allan Poe*, XVI, 306.
30. *Ibid.*, p. 307.
31. *The Complete Tales and Poems of Edgar Allan Poe*, p. 690.
32. *Ibid.*, p. 737.
33. *Ibid.*
34. *Ibid.*, p. 134.
35. *The Portable James Joyce*, p. 59.
36. *Ibid.*, p. 62, 64.
37. *Ibid.*, p. 66.
38. *Ibid.*
39. *Ulysses*, p. 656 *et passim* throughout Joyce's work and in all
Poe's tales on the sea and air.
40. *The Portable James Joyce*, p. 433-34.
41. *Ibid.*, p. 434.
42. *Ibid.*
43. *Ibid.*, p. 312.
44. *Ibid.*, p. 335. This image might be compared to "The Man of
the Crowd," in which the protagonist at first hesitates in his career,
but with a mad energy retraces his steps to the heart of the mighty
London.
45. *Ibid.*, p. 342.
46. *Ibid.*, p. 346.
47. *Ibid.*, p. 352.
48. *Ibid.*, p. 394.
49. *Ibid.*, p. 525.
50. *Ibid.*, p. 35.
51. *Ibid.*, p. 354.
52. *Ibid.*, p. 355.
53. *Ulysses*, pp. 582-83.
54. *The Complete Tales and Poems of Edgar Allan Poe*, p. 1011.
55. *The Portable James Joyce*, p. 351.
56. *Ibid.*, p. 431.
57. *Ibid.*, p. 421.
58. *Ibid.*, p. 352.
59. *Ulysses*, p. 145.

60. *Ibid.*, p. 677.
61. *The Complete Tales and Poems of Edgar Allan Poe*, p. 613.
62. *The Portable James Joyce*, p. 433.
63. *Ibid.*, p. 51.
64. *The Complete Tales and Poems of Edgar Allan Poe*, p. 672.
65. *Ibid.*, p. 654.
66. Harry Levin, *James Joyce: A Critical Introduction* (Norfolk, Conn.: New Directions, 1941), pp. 149-50.
67. *The Complete Tales and Poems of Edgar Allan Poe*, p. 239.
68. *Ibid.*, p. 626.
69. *The Portable James Joyce*, p. 394-95.
70. *Ibid.*, pp. 201-2.
71. *Ulysses*, p. 656.
72. Jean Paris, in *James Joyce par lui-même* (Paris: aux Éditions du Seuil, 1957), p. 106, quotes Marcel Brion, "Le thème de l'entrelacs et du labyrinthe dans l'oeuvre de Léonard de Vinci et leur signification," *Études d'Art*, No. 8-10 (1953-54).

Chapter Three

1. *Stephen Hero*, p. 86.
2. *Ibid.*, p. 80, and *The Portable James Joyce*, p. 479.
3. *The Complete Tales and Poems of Edgar Allan Poe*, p. 996.
4. *Ulysses*, p. 38.
5. *Finnegans Wake*, pp. 182-3.
6. *Ibid.*, p. 184.
7. *The Complete Works of Edgar Allan Poe*, XIV, 204.
8. Sir Desmond MacCarthy, *Memories* (New York: Oxford University Press, 1953), p. 120.
9. *The Complete Tales and Poems of Edgar Allan Poe*, p. 624-25.
10. *Ibid.*, p. 231.
11. *Ulysses*, p. 690.
12. *The Portable James Joyce*, p. 530.
13. *The Complete Tales and Poems of Edgar Allan Poe*, p. 246.
14. *The Portable James Joyce*, p. 142.
15. *Ibid.*, p. 494.
16. *Ibid.*, p. 403.
17. *The Complete Tales and Poems of Edgar Allan Poe*, p. 644.
18. *The Portable James Joyce*, p. 122.
19. *The Complete Works of Edgar Allan Poe*, XVI, 89.
20. *The Portable James Joyce*, p. 43.
21. *Ibid.*, p. 117.
22. *Ibid.*, pp. 44-45.
23. *Ibid.*, p. 521.

24. *The Complete Tales and Poems of Edgar Allan Poe*, p. 271, *et passim*.

25. *Ibid.*, p. 662.

26. *Stephen Hero*, p. 162.

27. *The Complete Tales and Poems of Edgar Allan Poe*, p. 144.

28. *The Portable James Joyce*, p. 191.

29. *Ibid.*, p. 46.

30. *Ibid.*, p. 82.

31. *Stephen Hero*, p. 162.

32. *Ulysses*, p. 108.

33. *The Complete Tales and Poems of Edgar Allan Poe*, p. 536.

34. *Ulysses*, p. 191.

35. *The Portable James Joyce*, p. 132.

36. *Ibid.*, p. 93.

37. Hugh Kenner, *Dublin's Joyce* (Bloomington: Indiana University Press, 1956), p. 338.

38. *Finnegans Wake*, p. 473.

39. *The Complete Tales and Poems of Edgar Allan Poe*, p. 650.

40. *Ibid.*, p. 613.

41. *The Portable James Joyce*, p. 187.

42. *Ibid.*, p. 227.

43. Frank Budgen, *James Joyce and the Making of Ulysses* (London: Grayson and Grayson, 1934), p. 93.

44. *Ulysses*, p. 38.

45. *The Complete Tales and Poems of Edgar Allan Poe*, p. 236.

46. *Ibid.*, p. 237.

47. *Ulysses*, p. 340.

48. *The Portable James Joyce*, p. 41.

49. *Ibid.*, p. 313.

50. *Ibid.*, p. 353.

51. *Ibid.*, p. 108.

52. *Ibid.*, p. 117.

53. Charles Baudelaire, *Les Oeuvres Complètes de Charles Baudelaire*, Vol. X (Paris: Louis Conrad, 1930), pp. 91-92.

54. *The Portable James Joyce*, p. 353.

55. *Ibid.*, p. 357.

56. *Ibid.*, p. 359.

57. *Ibid.*, p. 360.

58. *Ibid.*, p. 364.

59. *The Complete Tales and Poems of Edgar Allan Poe*, p. 460.

60. *Ibid.*, p. 526.

61. *Ulysses*, p. 567.

62. *Ibid.*, p. 582.

63. *The Complete Tales and Poems of Edgar Allan Poe*, p. 882.

64. *The Portable James Joyce*, p. 246.

Chapter Four

1. *The Complete Tales and Poems of Edgar Allan Poe*, p. 654.

2. Edward N. Davidson, *Poe: A Critical Study* (Cambridge: The Belknap Press of the Harvard University Press, 1957), p. 201.

2. *The Complete Tales and Poems of Edgar Allan Poe*, p. 640.

3. *Ibid.*, p. 752-53.

4. *Ibid.*, p. 810.

5. *Ibid.*, p. 664.

6. *Ibid.*

7. *Ibid.*, p. 665.

8. Davidson, p. 133.

9. *Ulysses*, p. 768.

10. Letter to Grant Richards written by James Joyce in Via Giovanni Boccaccio, Trieste, Austria, as published in Herbert Gorman, *James Joyce*, p. 150.

11. *Stephen Hero*, p. 146.

12. *The Portable James Joyce*, p. 119.

13. *Ibid.*

14. *Ibid.*, p. 50.

15. *Ibid.*, p. 52.

16. *Ibid.*, p. 58.

17. *Ibid.*, pp. 24-25.

18. *Ibid.*, p. 28.

19. Robert Stanley Ryf, "A Study of James Joyce's *A Portrait of the Artist*" (unpublshed Ph.D. dissertation, Columbia University,, 1956), p. 110.

20. *The Portable James Joyce*, p. 241.

21. *Ibid.*, p. 242.

22. Allen Tate, *The Forlorn Demon, Didactic and Critical Essays* (Chicago: Henry Regnery Co., 1953), p. 189.

23. *The Complete Tales and Poems of Edgar Allan Poe*, p. 654.

24. *The Portable James Joyce*, p. 28.

25. *Ibid.*, p. 641.

26. *Ibid.*, p. 627.

27. *Stephen Hero*, p. 194.

28. *Ibid.*

29. *The Portable James Joyce*, p. 288.

30. *Ibid.*, p. 313.

31. *Ibid.*, p. 493.

32. David Daiches, *The Novel and the Modern World* (Chicago: The University of Chicago Press, 1960), p. 81.

33. *The Portable James Joyce*, p. 520.

34. *The Complete Tales and Poems of Edgar Allan Poe*, p. 281.

35. *Ibid.*
36. *Ibid.*, p. 281.
37. *Ibid.*, XVI, 185.
38. *Ibid.*, pp. 185-86.
39. *Ibid.*, pp. 233-34.
40. *The Complete Tales and Poems of Edgar Allan Poe*, p. 875.
41. Charles Feidelson, *Symbolism in American Literature* (Chicago: University of Chicago Press, 1953), p. 40.
42. *The Complete Tales and Poems of Edgar Allan Poe*, p. 668.
43. *Ibid.*
44. Tate, p. 63.
45. Davidson, p. 189.
46. *The Complete Tales and Poems of Edgar Allan Poe*, pp. 305-6.
47. *Ibid.*, p. 284.
48. Magalaner and Kain, p. 77.
49. *The Complete Tales and Poems of Edgar Allan Poe*, p. 757.
50. *The Portable James Joyce*, p. 33.
51. *Ibid.*
52. *Ibid.*
53. *Ibid.*
54. *Ibid.*, p. 37.
55. *Ibid.*
56. *Ibid.*
57. *Ibid.*, p. 38.
58. *Ibid.*, pp. 647-48.
59. *Ibid.*, p. 259.
60. *Ibid.*, p. 394.
61. *Ibid.*, pp. 521-22.
62. *Ibid.*, p. 46.
63. *Ibid.*, p. 51.
64. *Ibid.*, p. 96.
65. *Ibid.*, p. 118.
66. *Ibid.*, p. 246.
67. *The Complete Tales and Poems of Edgar Allan Poe*, p. 762.
68. *Ibid.*, p. 875.
69. *The Portable James Joyce*, p. 421.
70. *Ibid.*, p. 423.
71. *Ibid.*, p. 429.
72. *Ulysses*, p. 10.
73. *The Complete Works of Edgar Allan Poe*, V, 449.
74. *Ibid.*, p. 663.
75. *Ibid.*, p. 689.
76. *Ibid.*, p. 294.
77. *Ibid.*, p. 649.

78. *Ibid.*, p. 615.

79. *Ibid.*, p. 683.

80. *Ibid.*, p. 633.

81. *Ibid.*, pp. 626 *et passim*.

82. Julian B. Kaye, "The Wings of Daedalus: Two Stories in 'Dubliners,'" *Modern Fiction Studies*, V (Spring, 1958), 40.

83. *The Portable James Joyce*, p. 233.

84. *Ibid.*, p. 39.

85. *Ibid.*, p. 42.

86. *Ibid.*, p. 46.

87. *Ibid.*, pp. 312-13.

88. *Ibid.*, p. 342.

89. *Ibid.*, pp. 349-50.

90. *Ibid.*, p. 334.

91. *Stephen Hero*, p. 77.

92. *The Complete Tales and Poems of Edgar Allan Poe*, p. 294.

93. *The Portable James Joyce*, pp. 429, 431.

94. *Ibid.*, p. 483.

95. *Ulysses*, p. 45.

Chapter Five

1. Patrick F. Quinn, *The French Face of Edgar Allan Poe* (Carbondale: Southern Illinois University Press, 1957), p. 253.

2. *The Complete Works of Edgar Allan Poe*, XIV, 195.

3. *Stephen Hero*, p. 211.

4. *Ibid.*, p. 186.

5. Frank Budgen, "Further Recollections of James Joyce," *Partisan Review*, XXIII (1956), 536.

6. Edgar Allan Poe, *Works*, XVI, 120, quoted by Nathan Bryllion Fagin in *The Histrionic Mr. Poe* (Baltimore: Johns Hopkins Press, 1949), p. 167.

7. *The Complete Works of Edgar Allan Poe*, XIV, 193.

8. Marshall McLuhan, "Joyce, Mallarmé, and the Press," *Sewanee Review*, LXII (Winter, 1954), 54-55.

9. William Y. Tindall, *James Joyce, His Way of Interpreting the Modern World* (New York: Charles Scribner's Sons, 1950), p. 30.

10. Paul Valéry, "Situation de Baudelaire," *Oeuvres* (Paris: Bibliothèque de la Pleiade, 1957), pp. 598-613.

11. *The Complete Works of Edgar Allan Poe*, XIV, 194.

12. *The Complete Tales and Poems of Edgar Allan Poe*, p. 681.

13. *The Portable James Joyce*, p. 251.

14. *The Complete Works of Edgar Allan Poe*, XIII, 148.

15. Emilie Noulet, *Paul Valéry*, études (ed. définitive; Bruxelles: La Renaissance du Livre, 1950), pp. 104-5.

16. Guy Michaud, in *Message Poétique du Symbolisme*, Librairie Nizet, Paris, 1947, I, 14, quotes "Enquête sur l'évolution littéraire" par J. Muret, *Echo de Paris*, XIV (Mars), 1891.

17. *The Complete Works of Edgar Allan Poe*, XIV, 207 and XVI, 28.

18. Hendry, p. 28.

19. Magalaner and Kain, p. 72.

20. Hayman, *James Joyce et Mallarmé*.

21. Édouard Dujardin, *Mallarmé, par un des siens* (Paris: Albert Messein, 1936), p. 45.

22. William York Tindall, *James Joyce: His Way of Interpreting the Modern World* (New York: Scribners, 1950), p. 40.

23. *The Portable James Joyce*, p. 472.

24. *Ibid.*, p. 426.

25. *Ibid.*, p. 471.

26. Gorman, p. 80.

27. *The Portable James Joyce*, p. 59.

28. *The Complete Tales and Poems of Edgar Allan Poe*, p. 306.

29. *The Portable James Joyce*, p. 304.

30. *The Complete Tales and Poems of Edgar Allan Poe*, pp. 893-94.

31. *The Portable James Joyce*, p. 479.

32. *The Complete Tales and Poems of Edgar Allan Poe*, pp. 665-66.

33. *Ibid.*, p. 678.

34. *Ibid.*, p. 641.

35. *The Portable James Joyce*, p. 473.

36. Jean Paris, *James Joyce Par Lui-même*, "Écrivains de toujours," aux Editions du Seuil, 1957, p. 58.

37. *The Portable James Joyce*, p. 71.

38. *The Complete Tales and Poems of Edgar Allan Poe*, p. 894.

39. Edward Callahan, Jr., "James Joyce's Early Esthetics: A Study of Its Origin and Function" (unpublished Ph.D. dissertation, The University of Wisconsin, 1956), p. 122.

40. *The Complete Tales and Poems of Edgar Allan Poe*, p.443.

41. *Ibid.*, p. 1007.

42. *Ibid.*, p. 1008.

43. Camille Mauclair, *Le Génie d'Edgar Poe* (Paris: Albin Michel, 1925), p. 278.

44. Stéphane Mallarmé, *Oeuvres Complètes*, "Crise des Vers," text established and annotated by Henri Mondor and G. Jean-Aubry (Paris: Gallimard, 1951), p. 366.

45. T. S. Eliot, "From Poe to Valéry," *Hudson Review*, II, No. 3 (Autumn, 1949), 337.

46. *The Complete Tales and Poems of Edgar Allan Poe*, p. 996.

47. *Oeuvres Complètes de Charles Baudelaire*, VII, 17.

48. *Ulysses*, p. 38.

49. Cecil Maurice Bowra, *The Romantic Imagination* (Cambridge: Harvard University Press, 1949), p. 192.

50. L. Maholy-Nagy, *Vision in Motion* (Chicago: Paul Theobald, 1947), p. 293.

51. *The Complete Tales and Poems of Edgar Allan Poe*, p. 657.

52. *Ibid.*, p. 458.

53. *Ibid.*, p. 770.

54. Étienne Henry Gilson, *Painting and Reality* (New York: Pantheon Books, 1957), p. 297, quoting Edgar Allan Poe, *The Complete Tales and Poems*, p. 893.

55. *The Portable James Joyce*, p. 426.

56. *Ibid.*, p. 364.

57. *Ibid.*, p. 426.

58. *Ulysses*, p. 628.

59. *Ibid.*, p. 270.

60. *The Portable James Joyce*, p. 42.

61. Davidson, p. 175.

62. *The Portable James Joyce*, p. 308.

63. *Ibid.*, p. 339.

64. *Ulysses*, p. 46.

65. *The Portable James Joyce*, p. 420.

66. *Stephen Hero*, p. 26.

67. *Ibid.*, p. 30.

68. Tindall, p. 67.

Chapter Six

1. George Snell, "First of the New Critics," *Quarterly Review of Literature*, II, No. 1 (Fall 1944), 339.

2. *The Portable James Joyce*, p. 227.

3. Frank Budgen, *James Joyce and the Making of Ulysses* (London: Grayson and Grayson, 1933), p. 92.

4. *Stephen Hero*, p. 37.

5. Anthony Bertram, *A Century of British Painting, 1851-1951* (London and New York: The Studio Publications, 1951), p. 64.

6. *Stephen Hero*, p. 33.

7. *The Portable James Joyce*, p. 478.

8. *Ibid.*, p. 478.

9. *Ibid.*

10. *Ibid.*, p. 482.

11. *Ibid.*, p. 257.

12. *Ibid.*, p. 426.

13. *Ibid.*, p. 256.

14. *Stephen Hero*, p. 211.
15. *The Portable James Joyce*, p. 342.
16. *Ulysses*, p. 371.
17. *Ibid.*, p. 49.
18. *The Portable James Joyce*, p. 57.
19. *Ibid.*, p. 267.
20. *Ibid.*, p. 59.
21. *Ibid.*, p. 322.
22. *Ibid.*, p. 268.
23. *Ibid.*, p. 427.
24. *Ibid.*, p. 427.
25. *Ibid.*, p. 271.
26. *Ibid.*, p. 455.
27. *Ibid.*, p. 251.
28. *Ibid.*, p. 74.
29. *Ibid.*, p. 56-57.
30. *Ibid.*, p. 59.
31. *Ibid.*, pp. 80-83.
32. *Ibid.*, pp. 193-94.
33. *Ulysses*, p. 184.
34. Frank Budgen, p. 42.
35. *Ulysses*, p. 49.
36. *The Portable James Joyce*, pp. 213-14.
37. *Ibid.*, p. 42.

Chapter Seven

1. Paul Valéry, "Au sujet d'Eurêka," *Oeuvres*, p. 861.
2. Herbert Read, "Surrealism and the Romantic Principle" in *Criticism: The Foundations of Modern Literary Judgment*, edited by Mark Schorer, Josephine Miles, and Gordon McKenzie (New York: Harcourt, Brace and Co., 1948), pp. 95 *et passim*.
3. *The Portable James Joyce*, p. 246.
4. *Ibid.*, pp. 433, 454.
5. Quinn, p. 245.
6. Istituto Italiano d'Arti Grafiche (Editore), *Arte Italiana del Nostro Tempo* (Bergamo, 1946), p. 26.
7. De Chirico, c. 1913 in James Thrall Soby, *Giorgio de Chirico* (New York: The Museum of Modern Art, 1954), p. 10.
8. Werner.Haftmann, *The Mind and Work of Paul Klee* (London: Faber and Faber, 1954), p. 140.
9. *The Portable James Joyce*, pp. 259-61.
10. *Ulysses*, p. 57.
11. *The Portable James Joyce*, pp. 21-22.
12. *Ibid.*, p. 19.

13. Hugo Münsterberg, *Twentieth Century Painting* (New York: Philosophical Library, 1951), p. 62.

14. *The Portable James Joyce*, p. 342.

15. *Ulysses*, p. 407.

16. *Ibid.*, p. 9.

17. *Ibid.*, p. 35.

18. *The Portable James Joyce*, p. 22.

19. James Thrall Soby and Alfred H. Barr, Jr., *Twentieth Century Italian Art* (New York: Museum of Modern Art, 1949), pp. 118-19.

20. *The Portable James Joyce*, p. 334.

21. *Ibid.*, p. 317.

22. *Ibid.*, pp. 252-53.

23. *Ulysses*, pp. 714-15.

24. *The Portable James Joyce*, p. 284.

25. *Ibid.*, p. 256-57.

26. *Ulysses*, p. 76.

27. *The Portable James Joyce*, p. 493.

28. *Ulysses*, p. 78.

29. Münsterberg, p. 61.

30. *The Portable James Joyce*, p. 33.

31. *Ibid.*, p. 507.

32. Kaye, p. 33.

33. André Breton, *Le Surréalisme et la Peinture* (New York: Brentano's, 1945), pp. 65-66.

Bibliography

APOLLINAIRE, GUILLAUME. *The Cubist Painters: Aesthetic Meditations.* New York: Wittenborn & Schultz, 1949.

BAAKE, JOSEF. *Das Riesenscherzbuch Ulysses.* Bonn: P. Hanstein, 1937.

BAUDELAIRE, CHARLES. *Oeuvres Complètes de Charles Baudelaire.* 2 vols. Paris: Louis Conard, 1930.

————. *Baudelaire on Poe: Critical Papers.* Translated and edited by Lois and Francis E. Hyslop, Jr. State College, Pennsylvania: Bald Eagle Press, 1952.

BEACH, JOSEPH WARREN. *The Twentieth Century Novel: Studies in Technique.* New York: Appleton-Century, 1932.

BERTRAM, ANTHONY. *A Century of British Painting, 1851-1951.* London and New York: The Studio Publications, 1951.

BISHOP, JOHN PEALE. "Finnegans Wake" in *Collected Essays.* Edited by Edmund Wilson. New York: Scribner's, 1948, pp. 146-65.

BLOCK, HASKELL M. "The Critical Theory of James Joyce," *Journal of Aesthetics and Art Criticism,* VIII (March, 1950), 172-84.

BONAPARTE, MARIE. *Édgar Poe.* Paris: Les Éditions Denoël et Steele, 1933.

BOWRA, C. M. *The Heritage of Symbolism.* London: Macmillan and Company, Ltd., 1947.

————. *The Romantic Imagination.* Cambridge: Harvard University Press, 1949.

BROOKS, VAN WYCK. *The World of Washington Irving.* New York: E. P. Dutton and Co., Inc., 1950.

BUDGEN, FRANK. *James Joyce and the Making of Ulysses.* London: Grayson and Grayson, 1934.

————. "Further Recollections of James Joyce," *Partisan Review,* XXIII (Fall, 1956), 530-44.

CALLAHAN, EDWARD F., JR. "James Joyce's Early Esthetic: A Study of Its Origin and Function." Unpublished Ph.D. dissertation, University of Wisconsin, 1957. (Microfilm.)

CAMPBELL, JOSEPH, and HENRY MORTON ROBINSON. *A Skeleton Key to Finnegans Wake.* New York: Harcourt, Brace, 1944.

CHENEY, SHELDON. *Expressionism in Art.* New York: Viking, 1934.

————. *The Story of Modern Art.* New York: Viking, 1941.

DAICHES, DAVID. *New Literary Values.* London: Oliver, 1936.

————. *The Novel and the Modern World*. Chicago: University of Chicago Press, 1960.

DAVIDSON, EDWARD H. *Edgar Allan Poe: A Critical Study*. Cambridge: The Belknap Press of Harvard University, 1957.

DUJARDIN, EDOUARD. *Le Monologue Intérieur: son apparition, ses origines, sa place dans l'oeuvre de James Joyce*. Paris: Messein, 1931.

————. *Mallarmé par un des siens*. Paris: Messein, 1936.

EDEL, LEON. *The Psychological Novel, 1900-1950*. Philadelphia: Lippincott, 1955.

EINSTEIN, CARL. *Die Kunst des 20. Jahrhunderts*. Berlin: Propylaen-Verlag, 1931.

ELIOT, T. S. "From Poe to Valéry," *Hudson Review*, II, no. 3 (Autumn, 1949), 327-42.

ENGSTROM, ALFRED G. "Poe, Leconte de Lisle and Tzara's Formula for Poetry," *Modern Language Notes*, LXXIII (1958), 435.

FAGIN, NATHAN BRYLLION. *The Histrionic Mr. Poe*. Baltimore: Johns Hopkins Press, 1949.

FEIDELSON, CHARLES. *Symbolism in American Literature*. Chicago: University of Chicago Press, 1953.

FRANK, JOSEPH. "Spatial Form in Modern Literature" in *Critiques and Essays on Modern Fiction*. Edited by John Aldridge. New York: Ronald Press, 1952, pp. 44-46.

FRIEDRICH, GERHARD. "The Gnomic Clue to James Joyce's Dubliners," *Modern Language Notes*, LXXII (June, 1957), 421-24.

GAFFÉ, RENÉ. *Giorgio de Chirico, le Voyant*. Bruxelles: La Boëtie, 1946.

GAUSS, EDWARD CHARLES. *The Aesthetic Theories of French Artists, 1855 to the Present*. Baltimore: Johns Hopkins Press, 1949.

GHEERBRANT, BERNARD. *James Joyce: Sa Vie, son Oeuvre, son Rayonnement*. Paris: La Hune, 1949.

GHISELIN, BREWSTER. "The Unity of Joyce's 'Dubliner,'" *Modern Fiction Studies*, IV (Spring, 1958), 31-41.

GILBERT, STUART. *James Joyce's Ulysses* (1930). 2nd ed. revised. New York: Knopf, 1952.

———— (ed.). *Letters of James Joyce*. New York: Viking Press, 1957.

GILSON, ÉTIENNE HENRY. *Painting and Reality*. New York: Pantheon Books, 1957.

GIVENS, SEON (ed.). *James Joyce: Two Decades of Criticism*. New York: Vanguard Press, 1948.

GORMAN, HERBERT. *James Joyce: His First Forty Years*. New York: Huebsch, 1924.

————. *James Joyce* (1940). Revised edition. New York: Rinehart, 1948.

GRIFFITH, CLARK. "Poe's Ligeia and the English Romantics," *University of Toronto Quarterly*, XXIV, No. 1 (October, 1954), 8-25.

HAFTMANN, WERNER. *The Mind and Work of Paul Klee*. London: Faber and Faber, 1954.

HATZFELD, HELMUT. *Literature Through Art*. New York: Oxford University Press, 1952.

HAYMAN, DAVID. *James Joyce et Mallarmé*. 2 vols. Paris: Lettres Modernes, 1956.

HENDRY, IRENE. "Joyce's Epiphanies" in *James Joyce: Two Decades of Criticism*. Edited by Seon Givens. New York: Vanguard Press, 1948.

HENTZE, RUDOLFE. *Die Proteische Wandlung im Ulysses von James Joyce und ihre Spiegelung im Stil*. Marburg: N. G. Elwertsche, 1933.

HIGHET, GILBERT. *The Classical Tradition*. New York and London. Oxford University Press, 1949.

HUTCHINS, PATRICIA. *Joyce's Dublin*. London: The Grey Wall Press, 1950.

————. *James Joyce's World*. London: Methuen, 1957.

HUYSMANS, JORIS-KARL. *À Rebours*. Bibliothèque Charpentier. Paris: Fasquelle Editeurs, n.d.

Istituto Italiano d'Arti Grafiche (editore). *Arte Italiana del Nostro Tempo*. Bergamo, 1946.

JOYCE, JAMES. *Chamber Music*. Edited by William York Tindall. New York: Columbia University Press, 1954.

————. *The Critical Writings of James Joyce*. Edited by Ellsworth Mason and Richard Ellmann. New York: The Viking Press, 1949.

————. *Finnegans Wake*. London: Faber and Faber, 1939.

————. *The Portable James Joyce*. New York: The Viking Press, 1958.

————. *Stephen Hero*. New York: A New Directions Book, 1955.

————. *Ulysses*. New York: The Modern Library, 1946.

JUNG, CARL G. *Die Wirklichkeit der Seele*. Zürich: Rascher Verlag, 1939.

KAIN, RICHARD M. *Fabulous Voyager: James Joyce's Ulysses*. Chicago: University of Chicago Press, 1947.

KAYE, JULIAN B. "The Wings of Daedalus: Two Stories in 'Dubliners,'" *Modern Fiction Studies*, IV (Spring, 1958), 31-41.

KENNER, HUGH. *Dublin's Joyce*. Bloomington: Indiana University Press, 1956.

————. "The Portrait in Perspective" in *James Joyce: Two Decades of Criticism*. Edited by Seon Givens. New York: Vanguard Press, 1948, pp. 175-90.

KÜHNELT, HARRO HEINZ. *Die Bedeutung von Edgar Allan Poe in der englischen Literatur.* Innsbruck: Universität Innsbruck, 1949.

————. "T. S. Eliot als Poe-Kritiker," *Die Neueren Sprachen*, V (1956), 105-12.

KUMAR, SHIV K. "Bergson and Stephen Dedalus' Aesthetic Theory," *Journal of Aesthetics and Art Criticism*, XVI (September, 1957), 124-27.

LAMAÎTRE, GEORGES. *From Cubism to Surrealism in French Literature.* Cambridge: Harvard University Press, 1941.

LEVIN, HARRY. *James Joyce: A Critical Introduction.* Norfolk, Conn.: New Directions, 1941.

————. *Contexts of Criticism.* Cambridge: Harvard University Press, 1957.

LOEHRICH, ROLF R. *The Secret of Ulysses: An Analysis of James Joyce's Ulysses.* McHenry, Illinois: Compass Press, 1953.

MACCARTHY, SIR DESMOND. *Memories.* New York: Oxford University Press, 1953.

MAGALANER, MARVIN. *A James Joyce Miscellany.* New York: James Joyce Society, 1957 and continuing.

————, and RICHARD M. KAIN. *Joyce: The Man, The Work, The Reputation.* New York: New York University Press, 1956.

MALLARMÉ, STÉPHANE. *Oeuvres Complètes.* Paris: Gallimard, 1951.

MAUCLAIR, CAMILLE. *The French Impressionists (1860-1900).* Translated by P. Konody. London: Duckworth and Co.; New York: E. P. Dutton and Co., n.d.

————. *Le Génie d'Edgar Poe.* Paris: Albin Michel, 1926.

MCLUHAN, MARSHALL. "Joyce, Mallarmé, and the Press," *Sewanee Review*, LXII (Winter, 1954), 38-55.

MERCANTON, JACQUES. *Poètes de l'univers.* Paris: Editions Albert Skira, 1947.

MICHAUD, GUY. *Message Poétique du Symbolisme.* Paris: Librairie Nizet, 1947.

MOHOLY-NAGY, L. *Vision in Motion.* Chicago: Paul Theobald, 1947.

MÜNSTERBERG, HUGO. *Twentieth Century Painting.* New York: Philosophical Library, 1951.

NOULET, ÉMILIE. *Paul Valéry.* Études. Bruxelles: La Renaissance du Livre, 1950.

PARIS, JEAN. *James Joyce par lui-même.* Paris: aux editions du Seuil, 1957.

POE, EDGAR ALLAN. *The Complete Works of Edgar Allan Poe.* 17 vols. Edited by James A. Harrison. New York: Society of English and French Literature, 1902.

————. *The Complete Tales and Poems of Edgar Allan Poe.* New York: The Modern Library, 1938.

POULET, GEORGES. "L'Univers Circonscrit d'Edgar Poe," *Les Temps Modernes*, X, Part 2 (January-July, 1955), 2179-2204.

POUND, EZRA. *Literary Essays*. Norfolk, Connecticut: New Directions, n.d.

———. *The Letters of Ezra Pound*. Edited by D. D. Paige. New York: Harcourt, Brace and Company, 1950.

QUINN, PATRICK FRANCIS. *The French Face of Edgar Poe*. Carbondale: Southern Illinois University Press; 1957.

RAYMOND, MARCEL. *De Baudelaire au Surréalisme*. Paris: José Corti, 1947.

RAYNAL, MAURICE. *Modern Painting*. Vol. III: *History of Modern Painting: From Picasso to Surrealism*. New York: Skira, 1950.

READ, HERBERT. "Surrealism and the Romantic Principle" in *Criticism: The Foundations of Modern Literary Judgment*. Edited by Mark Schorer, Josephine Miles, and Gordon McKenzie. New York: Harcourt, Brace and Co., 1948.

REWALD, JOHN. *The History of Impressionism*. New York: Museum of Modern Art, 1946.

ROTHSCHILD, EDWARD F. *The Meaning of Unintelligibility in Modern Art*. Chicago: University of Chicago Press, 1934.

RYF, ROBERT STANLEY. "A Study of James Joyce's *A Portrait of the Artist*." Unpublished Ph.D. dissertation, Columbia University, 1956. (Microfilm.)

SHANKS, EDWARD. *Edgar Allan Poe*. New York: The Macmillan Company, 1937.

SMIDT, KRISTIAN. *James Joyce and the Cultic Use of Fiction*. Oslo Studies in English, No. 4. Oxford: Basil Blackwell, 1955.

SNELL, GEORGE. "First of the New Critics," *Quarterly Review of Literature*, II, No. 1 (Fall, 1944), 339.

SOBY, JAMES THRALL. *Giorgio de Chirico*. New York: The Museum of Modern Art, 1954.

———, and ALFRED BARR, JR. *Twentieth Century Italian Art*. New York: The Museum of Modern Art, 1949.

STARKIE, ENID. *From Gautier to Eliot. The Influence of France on English Literature 1851-1939*. London: Hutchinson, 1960.

STOLL, ELMER EDGAR. *From Shakespeare to Joyce*. New York: Doubleday, Doran and Co., Inc., 1944.

STRONG, L. A. G. *The Sacred River: An Approach to James Joyce*. London, 1949.

SYMONS, ARTHUR. *Figures of Several Centuries*. London: Constable & Co., Ltd., 1916.

———. *The Symbolist Movement in Literature*. New York: E. P. Dutton and Co., 1919.

TATE, ALLEN. *The Forlorn Demon: Didactic and Critical Essays.* Chicago: Henry Regnery Co., 1953.

——. "Three Commentaries," *Sewanee Review,* LVIII (Winter, 1950), 10-15.

THOMPSON, FRANCIS. *Literary Criticisms.* Newly discovered and collected by Rev. Terence L. Connolly. New York: E. P. Dutton and Co., Inc., 1948.

TINDALL, WILLIAM YORK. *Forces in Modern British Literature, 1885-1946.* New York: Knopf, 1947.

——. *James Joyce: His Way of Interpreting the Modern World.* New York: Scribner's, 1950.

——. "James Joyce and the Hermetic Tradition," *Journal of the History of Ideas,* XV (January, 1954), 23-39.

——. *The Literary Symbol.* New York: Columbia University Press, 1955.

USSHER, ARLAND. *Three Great Irishmen: Shaw, Yeats, and Joyce.* London: Gollancz, 1952.

VALÉRY, PAUL. *Oeuvres.* Paris: Bibliothèque de la Pleiade, 1957.

VERLAINE, PAUL. *Les Poètes Maudits.* Paris: Léon Vannier, 1884.

——. *Oeuvres Complètes de Paul Verlaine.* Vol. IV. Paris: Albert Messein, éditeur, 1926.

WILDI, MAX. "Arthur Symons als Kritiker der Literatur," *Anglistische Forschungen.* Heft 67. Dissertation, Heidelberg, 1929.

WILENSKI, R. H. *Modern French Painters.* New York: Harcourt, 1949.

WILSON, EDMUND. *Axel's Castle: A Study in the Imaginative Literature of 1870-1930.* New York: Scribner's, 1931.

Index